REDISCOVERING
OUR
SPIRITUAL
GIFTS

REDISCOVERING OUR SPIRITUAL GIFTS

*Building Up the Body
of Christ
Through the Gifts of
the Spirit*

Charles V. Bryant

UPPER
ROOM BOOKS®
NASHVILLE

REDISCOVERING OUR SPIRITUAL GIFTS
Revised Edition

© 1991 by Charles V. Bryant. All rights reserved.

Cover design: Cindy Helms
Cover illustration: Richard Cook
Book design: Thelma Whitworth
Seventh Printing: 2001

Library of Congress Catalog Card Number: 90-71865
ISBN: 0-8358-0633-2

Printed in the United States of America on acid-free paper

TO
MY GRANDCHILDREN
Adrienne, Adam, Vanessa, Ariel
Olivia, Brandon, Michael,
and Sarah Jane

Contents

Foreword

A cautionary word to the reader—a forewarning, if you will: This book could revolutionize your concept of Christianity, make a positive difference in your commitment to Christ and the church, and protect you from "spiritual burnout."

Well-crafted and thoroughly researched, this presentation of spiritual gifts is part of the growing evidence that the charismatic renewal movement of the sixties and seventies is maturing in healthy, helpful expressions in mainline churches.

Dr. Charles V. Bryant has written a very practical book, informational as well as formational, designed to assist the Christian in discovering his or her particular spiritual gifts and to give guidance for building up the body of Christ through the gifts of the Spirit.

The New Testament is clear that in addition to inviting us to be members of the body of Christ, the Holy Spirit graciously gives each of us special energies and tools for ministry called gifts (*charismata*). Having a gift of the Spirit is not a mark of Christian maturity; the goal is rather to employ that gift for the glory of God and the mutual good of the community.

Rediscovering Our Spiritual Gifts could well become a needed handbook for local church nomination and personnel committees who are charged with the sacred task of recruiting church leadership. Too often the mindset consists of simply finding a warm body to fill a vacant position rather than asking the crucial question: Who in the church has the particular spiritual gifts needed to do this particular job?

9

Readers will find especially valuable the two exercises for identifying their personal gifts of the Spirit. This is also an excellent text for group study. Paul's counsel to the Corinthian church is restated throughout the pages of this vital volume, a word waiting to be sounded in the church today:

Now concerning spiritual gifts, brothers and sisters,
I do not want you to be uninformed.
—1 Corinthians 12:1, NRSV

JAMES K. WAGNER

Introduction

In the spring of 1982, I began to scheme an exit from the ministry. I would be giving up a calling and practice that began in 1954. I had done nearly everything I hoped to do in response to what I believed to be a genuine calling. I made many mistakes along the way, more than I wanted to. I enjoyed many successes, more than I deserved. Many people complimented my work; others complemented my efforts with their appropriate responses. I had every reason to continue.

Yet, I was miserable. I was burned out. I wanted out! My spiritual condition had declined to a professional management of an institution, the church, for which I was losing respect. I was just pulling time and getting by with as little as possible. At the time, I rarely read the Bible for personal spiritual nourishment, and I rarely prayed. For me, such exercises were too uneventful to take seriously.

Then something happened. On a rainy Saturday afternoon, I was returning from my weekly day off, dreading the chores and hypocrisy of leading others in worship the next morning. I was driving an automobile with no radio when boredom caused me to look around to find something to glance-read while driving. I spotted on the passenger's seat a tape player and two tapes that two persons had left with my secretary with instructions to get me to listen to them. I already had a shoe box full of tapes that well-meaning people had given me over the years. Nothing excited me about them, so I tucked them away. Here were two more, and I was bored enough to try anything. I listened to the first one—but for only five minutes. I couldn't finish it then because I began crying so hard I couldn't concentrate.

The tape was a testimony of a businessman who had been reclaimed by God and restored to an exciting relationship and service at fifty-two years of age. He and I were the same age. As he described his boring and empty life as a Christian and how God encountered him, turned him around, and gave him a new spiritual lease on life, I began to weep. I could not remember the last time I had shed a tear. In fact, I had concluded something was so dreadfully wrong with me that I could never cry again. Was I wrong!

I managed to get home through my veil of tears without an accident and began to "have it out" with God. I had given up on God's active presence long ago. Many times, while driving home from church, I shouted in anger, "God, where were you? I was there doing my thing. What did you do today?" That afternoon I was down on my knees doing the talking, and God was still silent. I wanted to hear a voice. I wanted a sign. I wanted anything from God that could shed light on what was happening. Nothing came forth, except more tears.

In general, a pastor is in a peculiar and precarious position when something like this happens. If an experience like this is shared with the wrong parishioner, one's credibility and effectiveness are shot. Most church members want to think their pastor walks on water. If one tells a colleague, the rumor mill works overtime to indicate emotional sickness. If one goes to a superintendent (supervisor) or bishop, the next appointment is jeopardized. So, one is left alone with God. That's where I was for eight full weeks, horrible weeks, "in the hands of an angry God," I thought!

During my wilderness experience, God silently and mysteriously exposed me to me. I didn't like what I saw, what I had become. It was like going to hell and meeting the enemy, discovering that hell is within and "the enemy is me." God gave me just enough curiosity to stick out the battle to see the outcome. Then divine power made an obvious move.

I had had enough. I wanted no more. I was tired of the whole thing. I had cried enough for ten persons. I was dry. I was ready to admit total depravity, defeat, mental illness—anything to get relief. Around midnight, while lying on my back on the floor after praying until I was exhausted, I gave up. I told God that I didn't want to live another hour. I didn't want to see the sun rise again. I told God that life was worthless, and that I was worse. I didn't deserve to live another minute, didn't want to live another minute, and daylight should not be wasted on me another day. Then it happened.

In the pitch darkness of that night and room, a room without any light coming into it, I saw something dark move upward through my body and out through the top of my head. It was silent but moving. I saw it hover and disappear. Suddenly, I received a peace, a serenity, that I never thought possible. The peace was so powerful, so beautiful, so real, that I wanted it to last forever. I enjoyed a delicious sleep for the balance of the night.

I heard no voice or instructions and saw no signs—except what left in the darkness. When the new day began, a new life was restored to me. Many, many things began to change. Almost without effort, I took a 180-degree turn. I will not bore you with details. I do want to say that the Bible, prayer, and other books took on a new fascination for me to help me find out what happened and was happening to me.

I eventually came across the book *Body Life* by Ray Stedman that opened the door to a new understanding of myself and the church as the body of Christ. A professor of physics at a university where I served a church as pastor had given me the book in 1975. I humored him, as I did the others who gave me tapes, and sent him on his way with my thanks. I put the book in my library and forgot it until something divine moved me to read it—seven years later!

It was like discovering a long-lost map that leads to an indescribable treasure. The book describes how the church has neglected its divine structuring in favor of a secular model that has not worked, does not work, and never will work for vital life. That book opened up for me a new dimension for understanding how the church works as a spiritual force through the *charismata*. Thus, my new life was launched with a mission to tell the story to others.

I am proposing in this book a serious study of the extraordinary powers God gives to people who receive the Holy Spirit. These powers are manifestly present in the discovery, development, and deployment of spiritual gifts by which we are able to be more (in the Spirit) than what we are (in the flesh) and to do more (in the Spirit) than what we can (in the flesh).

My study of the spiritual gifts gives me opportunities for Christian service I never dreamed possible. I have conducted over three hundred workshops for Lutherans, Disciples of Christ, Presbyterians, United Methodists, and Moravians throughout the United States, taught in universities, preached revivals based on discovering the gifts, and held numerous retreat seminars for pastors. I am realizing how open and eager Christians are to discover and claim ministries that are designed by God for them.

Unfortunately, in the mainline churches this study of specific gifts for ministry has not had the attention that could have made our history different. But that is changing. I see a new "early church" awakening, not as we thought it would happen some three or four decades ago through revivals and decisions for Christ, but in a deeper exposure to and study of the manifestations of the Holy Spirit and the charismatic structuring of church ministries.

The early period of the New Testament church was one with vital expressions of effective ministry, structured by the free and directive power of the Holy Spirit. Under the Holy Spirit's direction and gifting, the church was a highly visible community-type organism, one made up of complementary and harmonizing parts, but parts which were distinctively and functionally different. Paul directed his attention to these different parts or gifts in Romans 12, 1 Corinthians 12, and Ephesians 4, and he did so mainly because of prevailing ignorance and abuse of the gifts. He never made any effort to justify or defend the *charismata*.

Subsequent history shows us how far Christians drifted from the direct endowment of the Holy Spirit. While the early church was made up of Spirit-filled or endowed persons, by the end of the first century a division began to be apparent. A priesthood of special persons dominated an unpriestly laity, the former having special qualities and privileges granted under the authority of institutional leaders. This, despite the New Testament teaching that the whole new people of God are a priesthood ministering to one another for edification and the whole body ministering to the whole world.

The charismatic structuring for edification (building up) and mission (outreach) began to erode severely when a clear-cut division between clergy and laity became official toward the end of the second century. Intrigue toward the Holy Spirit and the "experience" of empowering gave way to doctrines, creeds, and theologies about the Holy Spirit. This prevailed until the sixteenth century when a new breakthrough came as the result of personal conversion and the enlightenment of the Holy Spirit. Assailed by the explosive force of this "new wine," church organizational structures swayed and tottered and gave way to new churches coming to birth, the Bible replaced dusty creeds, and men wrote new theologies. It was nothing less than a Reformation. Its authentic spiritual power spread throughout the whole church, as the church, in the following centuries, spread out to the whole world with the good news.

A more recent and significant result was that sometime in the 1950s this all came to an apex when laypeople of all cultures, races, and denominations suddenly became aware that they were not second-class citizens in God's kingdom. Something happened to them that could only be explained as an outpouring of God's Spirit. And with that Spirit, certain extraordinary spiritual powers became manifest. To be sure, this was not confined to laypersons. Pastor and priest also realized new power. It came to the attention of all that the special graces did not belong only to an ordained clergy.

By the 1970s, such a wind was blowing—at first called Neo-Pentecostalism and then the "charismatic movement"—that many church leaders and pastors began to open themselves to the possibility of something far beyond just another religious fad. A new hope for "meaning in life" and the "real spiritual part of religion" was born.

This new hope lay in the rediscovery that God's people are one. All members of the body of Christ are to be treated and respected with equal charismatic ranking, never as one over another but all as servants in ministry to and with everyone else (Rom. 12:3-5).

When people open themselves to God, they find that an experience of the Spirit of God is inseparable from the discovery and exercise of the charismata, the gifts. Such should never be a threat to any church body that seeks to lift up the church as the body of Christ in and for the world. Nor should the exercise of the gifts threaten any church official.

We are increasingly aware of a charismatic renewal growing within the mainline churches. And where this is happening, new vigor and growth are taking place. The charismatic movement of the 1950s is not going away. We must not want it to leave because of what is happening as a

15

result. Laypersons are experiencing the reality of the Spirit in their lives in such a way that peculiar abilities and power for Christian services are surfacing. They are viewing this new experience as gifts for ministry, not as an opportunity to display and engage in emotional "orgies" as was reported in some quarters during the initial phase of the movement.

I yearn to assist others in discovering the powerful and extraordinary gifts God has given them. These gifts will make their lives more meaningful, eventful, serviceable, and productive as Christians. I can guarantee this.

Gifts are powerful. They work when they are worked. We may never see the results or reap the harvest. Yet, there is great joy in believing and hoping someday someone's life may be touched and tamed by a gift of ministry faithfully used.

Gifts are innumerable. Their variety is as wide as our acceptance. Let us not limit them with small faith or smother them with popular trends and techniques. We've tried nearly everything else to revitalize the church; now let's try God's way—the gifts. Paul said, "Now we have received not the spirit of the world, but the Spirit which is from God, *that we might understand* the gifts bestowed on us by God" (1 Cor. 2:12, emphasis mine).

I offer this book as a gift to persons who want to know more about the spiritual gifts and as an aid to their gifts' discovery. Two special features include (1) the description of behavioral characteristics for thirty-two gifts and (2) the presentation of two ways to discover one's gifts—a process called O.B.E.D.I.E.N.C.E. and a Grace-Gifts Discovery Inventory. Together, they offer a unique venture into a new and promising understanding of one's spirituality and position in the body of Christ.

1

The Meaning and Scope of Spiritual Gifts

We often limit and cripple the church's effectiveness when we overlook or sidestep the choices, power, and guidance of God through the Holy Spirit. We are afraid to yield our big, impersonal institution—local church or denomination—to the dynamic and unpredictable force we know as the Holy Spirit. We say we believe in the Holy Spirit, but we find it difficult to yield to the Spirit. So, out of ignorance and confusion, perhaps distrust, about the mysterious operations of the Spirit, the easier and safer direction is to continue using our God-given intelligence and judgments.

Current needs and spiritual powers always form the active agenda of the Holy Spirit. That is why the church must be open to assignments, appointments, and charges from God. There is no other way to get back to, or to move forward to, the unity and bond of fellowship unique to the authentic body of Christ. Paul reminds us,

> You lack no single gift while you wait expectantly for our Lord Jesus Christ to be revealed. God will keep you firm to the end, without reproach on the day of our Lord Jesus Christ. God, alone, calls you to share in the life of Jesus Christ our Lord; and God is faithful.
>
> —1 Corinthians 1:7-9, AP

The Biblical Meaning and Scope

Four biblical passages specifically deal with spiritual gifts: Romans 12:1-8; 1 Corinthians 12:1-31; Ephesians 4:1-16; and 1 Peter 4:10-11.

Although these differ textually and contextually, they form a unity of meaning that cements together the church's twofold ministry. The church ministers to itself for health and wholeness, often called edification in the Bible (see Eph. 4:12). The church also ministers to all people; we call this service. In these passages, listing some twenty spiritual gifts, we discover certain principles to help us understand the importance of gifts.

1. **The gifts are for service.** They are not for personal adornment, status, power, or popularity. They enable us to do effective service for the body of Christ, the church, and, through the church, the world.

The biblical word for "service" is *diakonia,* and it refers to something done with *agape* love (see 1 Cor. 13). First Peter 4:10-11 declares "As each has received a gift, employ it for one another . . . in order that in everything God may be glorified through Jesus Christ." First Corinthians 12:7 says it another way: "To each is given the manifestation of the Spirit for the common good." Ephesians 4:12 states that the gifts were for "building up the body of Christ."

Gifts are not personal property or natural qualities to be used as we wish. They are divine energy creating, molding, and directing new abilities for special ministries to the world through the church (see John 3:16).

2. **God assigns and empowers the gifts.** Our desire for certain gifts does not guarantee our acquisition of them. It's like wanting to be taller or to have more hair; we cannot do anything about it. Perhaps at this point we need to clear up a misunderstanding that comes from an unfortunate translation of 1 Corinthians 12:31.

In the Greek language, the mood of some verbs cannot be determined except by the context. In the passage cited, the verb translated "desire" or "aim at" has only two moods, indicative and imperative. An early translator arbitrarily chose the imperative form, and others followed suit. Now take a look at the problem Paul was addressing. It was the invidious, self-seeking, and disruptive use of certain gifts. Translating "desire" or "aim at" in the indicative instead of the imperative would be more consistent with the context. The new statement would be, "So you yearn for the best there is! Well, let me tell you what it is." Then Paul launches into his examination of *agape* love, which is the governing power behind all gifts. Actually, comprehending the import of the thirteenth chapter of

1 Corinthians requires considering the twelfth and fourteenth chapters; the whole section has to do with understanding and properly using gifts.

This explanation is in concert with the other related passages: "Having gifts that differ according to the grace *given* to us" (Rom. 12:6, emphasis mine); "It is the same God who *inspires* [or breathes into] them all in every one" (1 Cor. 12:6, emphasis mine); "All these are inspired by one and the same Spirit, who *apportions* to each one individually as he wills" and "God has *appointed* in the church" (1 Cor. 12:11, 28, emphasis mine).

Another point we must not overlook is that God, not the individual or the community of Christians, chooses our gifts. We are not, as it were, standing in a spiritual gifts cafeteria with a tray in hand picking out the gifts we want as we move along the counter. No, God designs and distributes the gifts according to divine wisdom, not human petitions (see 2 Cor. 13:14). God alone knows what we need for the "building up the body of Christ" and the "common good" of the church (see Eph. 4:12; 1 Cor. 12:7).

3. **All Christians are included.** Everyone is gifted for special ministries. Although some people say they aren't, they may be thinking about talents or natural abilities. Some even excuse themselves from serving the church because they claim the absence of usable talents and skills. But the biblical truth is that all Christians have spiritual gifts that carry extraordinary powers and responsibilities.

4. **Only God knows the limit to the variety of gifts.** This statement should not introduce confusion over choices because God makes the choice. Paul's differing lists suggest to me that his readers knew this. Paul addressed himself only to the neglected and abused gifts. I do not believe he attempted to make an exhaustive list. Because we can count only twenty or so in the passages cited does not mean that God limits us to that number. The only limitation comes from our ignorance, resistance, and rejection concerning the operations of the Holy Spirit (see Eph. 4:30; 1 Thess. 5:19).

The Corinthians limited themselves to certain spectacular or sensational gifts, such as tongues, miracles, healings, and prophecy. You can imagine what a shock it was when Paul mentioned other gifts, such as interpretation of tongues, discerning of spirits, wisdom, knowledge, helps, and administration. Those gifts, to them, had no status and commanded little interest compared with emotional ecstasies and dramatic miracles.

Notice also that it obviously did not occur to Paul to tell them that the gifts they were using were wrong. He scored them heavily and sarcastically over something else. They ignored and neglected the quieter and more obscure gifts, which were just as essential, if not more so, to the fullness of Christian fellowship and ministry (see 1 Cor. 12:22-25).

This point is even more impressive in Romans 12, where it is difficult to determine the end of Paul's list of gifts. He mentions other qualities of Christian behavior that cannot be limited to the clergy and other leaders in the local church. He speaks to all members of the church.

A last point concerns the way the Book of Ephesians takes the teaching about gifts to the ultimate: the purpose of the gifts is to bring the church to full maturity "in Christ." This maturity cannot take place among disconnected or isolated individuals, or within a corporate body that overlooks the well-being and participation of the individuals who make up the body. The author of this epistle shows how every part of the body is intricately, intimately, and vitally connected with, through, and under Christ as head.

5. **The use of gifts determines health and growth.** The church is a single organism made up of many parts. Paul makes this clear by using the human anatomy as a model. The church has organs and systems, each of which is unique in size, shape, position, and function. The health of the whole body depends on the health and proper functioning of the individual parts. The body can never afford to neglect or discount the position and function of any organ, despite its size or distance from the head. Also, for health's sake, no individual part can overlook the value of the whole body.

Paul uses this anatomical analogy to describe our relationship with Christ. Christ, as the head, fits and connects all individuals together with equality in value, although each is different in function. Christ enables us as a corporate body to sustain growth with the power of love (see Eph. 4:11-16).

To summarize, Paul's metaphorical use of the body of Christ to describe the church and its ministry includes several dimensions. God designs and commissions us for ministry through the gifts. Mutual interdependence undergirds these ministries. The Holy Spirit energizes and directs these ministry gifts toward a wholeness in Christ. Paul, under the guidance of the Holy Spirit, sets before us the challenge of a vital spiritual fellowship. This fellowship is made vital only through an every-member participation in ministry. It matures in Christ only as the members live and serve by the standard of *agape* love.

Meaning and Scope Beyond the Bible: Spiritual, Physical, Psychological, and Social Dimensions

A complete understanding of Christian living does not divide a person into parts. Though Christians are extraordinarily spiritual, they are physical, psychological, and social beings. Here is where we hit a snag. Many Christians view life as primarily spiritual. Perhaps they follow the model of others. For example, many athletes consider the physical the most important dimension, some psychologists overemphasize human thinking and behavior, and sociologists often give first rank to relational behavior and systems. The truth is that we are unfair to ourselves when we identify any of these as all-important unless we favor one for research or therapy. These broad categories help us to relate to ourselves, to God, to others, and to our environment. Each facet is essential to the attainment of a full and happy life.

Yet, many persons are highly suspicious of a study pertaining to the spiritual nature of human beings. This attitude comes from the rapid achievements in the physical sciences. Although the physical sciences are still in their infancy, many of us in the Western world tend to subordinate nearly everything to them, even psychology and religion.

A look at history shows us that the church was born out of a high regard for the spiritual nature of humanity. Nevertheless, a world view, developed by Aristotle and incorporated in religion by Thomas Aquinas, created a suspicion toward anything that purports to be essentially spiritual. This perspective may be one reason the church has problems dealing with and sorting out what it believes about and can legitimately experience of the Holy Spirit.

A scientifically and physically oriented culture downplays a purely spiritual power or influence. Such a physicalistic world view attempts to reduce all events to lawful interactions of matter and energy within a spatiotemporal context; nothing else deserves attention. This approach also maintains that eventually and inevitably all so-called spiritual experiences can and probably will be measured as mere physical forces exclusively contained in a person's nervous system.

Some people claim that when one has a profound life-changing experience, such as conversion, it is conceivable that an electrode applied to a certain spot on the brain could just as easily produce the same results. For a long time now, some behavioral psychologists have claimed that certain psychochemical drugs produce and sustain "spiritual" states normally and historically associated with the active spirit and grace of God.

The argument for this view depends on modern science—still in its infancy, mind you—and what it has discovered and done for us. I believe, however, someday, under the grace of God, we will discover something. We will understand that our ignorance, not our intelligence, creates and maintains these artificial divisions between spiritual, physical, psychological, and social. In addition, compartmentalizing of life causes ill health—spiritual, psychological, physical, and social.

An understanding of the charismatic nature of our relationship with God can help us here. This giftedness of God's grace reveals just how unitary and whole we are, although differing in quality and quantity. This biospirituality blends all dimensions into a sacred wholeness that cannot be measured or described merely by spiritual or physical means.

Though Christians are rooted and grounded in the common soil of humanity, they are also spiritual beings with an extrasensory reality. This intimate reality offers an experience of new power (*dunamis*) in life. It brings new meanings, new motivations, and new fulfillment to the mental, physical, and social dimensions. Second Corinthians 5:17 describes it as a new humanity, a significant part of which concerns spiritual gifts. Paul's discourse on the gifts in 1 Corinthians 12 elaborates on this new source of authentic living, which is in Jesus Christ, "our wisdom, our righteousness and sanctification and redemption" (1 Cor. 1:30).

To the early Christians, their human nature, physical universe, and social relations were extraordinarily endowed with the grace (*charis*) of God. The indwelling Holy Spirit, or the inner reality of the living Christ, caused them to view life differently than they had. That is why Paul said "unspiritual" persons do not "receive the gifts [*charismata*]" (1 Cor. 2:14).

"Receive" here comes from a Greek word that really means "grasp through the senses." The gifts are so much a part of God that no one can approximate their manifestations without the grace of God. Although the early Christians did not consider themselves superior to or better than others, they experienced a new life in Christ that was superior to and better than the former life. The unbelievers neither displayed nor understood this transformation (see John 9:24-32).

According to Paul, this gifted life of Christians includes special wisdom and understanding that no amount of worldly wisdom can offer or alter (see 1 Cor. 6:2-16). Even our speaking or explaining cannot be comprehended by those whose source of real living is not Jesus Christ. This is one reason for the great gap between the purists in the physicalistic world view and the others (some of whom are scientists) who experience reality in terms of being in Christ.

Yet, as biospiritually alive and wise persons, we cannot divorce ourselves from the boundaries and limitations of our humanity—our physical, psychological, and social characteristics. What we actually experience in this grace (giftedness) of God transcends the difference between spirit and matter. It is similar to the principle of synergism: the whole is greater than the sum of the parts. Spiritual gifts faithfully received and obediently used affect the intimate relationship between the psychological, physical, and social traits of the human personality.

The acknowledged presence and use of grace gifts unavoidably affect our behavior, attitudes, outlook, motivations, and relationships. And the physical body cannot help being influenced. This does not mean that we become physically stronger, taller, and more intellectual because of the spiritual gifts. It does mean that the mind and the body become the recipients of a divine presence that translates into extraordinary means for an individualized ministry to others and an improved self-esteem.

Each Christian has a personality or disposition colored by the specific gifts present and practiced. The combination of gifts and their various manifestations determine how a person acts in relation to self and others in the body of Christ. These behavioral traits of the specific gifts are described in detail in subsequent chapters. Many Christians, if not most, practice their gifts without being consciously aware of them. Usually after two years of growth, serious converts to Christ find a ministry consistent with their gifts—without knowing it. I have heard many persons tell how their work for Christ was joy-filled, but they didn't know why until they discovered that all along they were working out of their gifts. A seventy-year-old man gave an emotional testimony after a workshop where he discovered one of his gifts. He said, "All my life I knew there was something I really enjoyed doing for Christ and the church. But I've always had a tinge of guilt, thinking that I was doing my thing for self-gratification. This morning, while I was shaving and praying about the gifts, God revealed to me that what I had been doing and enjoying all along was coming out of my gift. I got so excited about it that I could hardly finish shaving without cutting myself. I've been singing all day long. And to think that I have felt guilty over the joy of doing what God wanted me to do!"

A final point is that the discovery and the use of spiritual gifts cure burnout. This problem plagues many professions, occupations, and volunteer organizations. The main cause of burnout is the loss of motivation, and the result is ineffectiveness or apathy.

I have learned that the solution to burnout in the church, for the laity and the clergy, is the discovery and the use of spiritual gifts. When persons serve because of guilt, because of the desire to escape from boredom or to please or appease others, or because no one else will do it, burnout is inevitable. When they serve because of their gifts, they do not burn out. They may *wear* out, but they will not burn out. The gifts are endowments of specialized energy from the Holy Spirit. With this new energy come renewed motivation and a new self-esteem related to God's will (see Rom. 12:1-2).

Also, a new confidence about place and function in the body of Christ causes one to accept responsibilities without a sensitivity toward being used or manipulated by others. The gifted person's level of enthusiasm rises to embrace a positive attitude toward difficult or impossible odds. This new person in Christ becomes more than he or she is—in the flesh—and can do more—in the Spirit—than unspiritual mortals can do.

24

2

The Source and Resources of Spiritual Gifts

The Source

Are the gifts from the Holy Spirit? On this point, Paul helps us and confuses us, too. He wrote only about problematic and critical issues that were immediate. He did not cover many things that he and his readers took for granted. We have to make inferences to get to them. Besides, Paul had the special gift of knowledge (*gnosis*) by which he revealed mysteries God unveiled only to him (see Col. 1:24-29). Also, because of our different languages, lack of information, and place in time, we are not clear about many things he taught as vital to Christian living.

The lack of specificity for the source of the gifts is an illustration. In Ephesians 4 Paul says that Christ is the giver of the gifts. In another passage he declares that God inspires (breathes in) the gifts and that their manifestations are of the Spirit (see 1 Cor. 12:6-7). Then, too, Paul states that the work of grace is the means by which God gives us the gifts (see Rom. 12:6). Some students use Paul as textual proof for the doctrine of the Trinity because of his use of the terms *Spirit, Lord,* and *God* (see 1 Cor. 12:4-6). My belief is that Paul's emphasis here is on the gifts (*charismata*) and not on three persons of the Trinity.

I am a unitary human being. Yet, as son, husband, and father, I am radically and dramatically different. As a son, I cannot relate to my parents in any other way than as a son. It is impossible for me to view my mother as I do my wife. My relationship with my wife is altogether different. There is no way I can view my wife the same as my mother. I

25

am a father of four daughters, and it is impossible for me to regard them in any other way than as a father. Although I am the same human being, my parents, wife, and daughters do not view me as the same. I view them and express myself in three distinctive ways. Yet, I am I and no other—undivided—with the same physical, mental, and emotional equipment I use in all three roles. Whatever I am, whoever I am, my indivisible self manifests itself differently according to the relationship.

Somehow, this concept helps me to understand God's three basic expressions we know as the Trinity. It's the same divine person expressing self in three different ways: God as Father, God as Son, and God as Spirit.

When someone asks who gives the gifts, I answer, "According to scripture, God is the giver; according to scripture, Christ is the giver; and according to scripture, the Holy Spirit is the giver." The gifts are not merely Holy Spirit-gifts. They are God-gifts, Christ-gifts, and Spirit-gifts.

Our confusion often comes from calling them spiritual gifts. The adjective *spiritual* makes a point of their not coming from a physical source. Because they are spiritual does not mean they come from the Spirit and not God or Christ.

First Corinthians 2:9-16 offers a reason for receiving the Holy Spirit we seldom, if ever, consider. Paul elaborates on 1:30: "He is the source of your life in Christ Jesus, whom God made our wisdom, our righteousness and sanctification and redemption." Then he unfolds God's design for redemption in Christ Jesus as a wisdom hidden until now. He undauntingly unveils something that "*no* eye has seen, *nor* ear heard, *nor* the heart of man conceived" (emphasis mine). What boldness!

In verse 10 he indicates the connection between God and Spirit. They are not separate beings. The Spirit is a specific activity of God. In verse 11 Paul shows God's reflection on divine selfhood by using *pneuma* or "Spirit" to describe the part of divine activity that has no human or material origin. Then he explains in verse 12 that this divine disclosure becomes a vital part of our human experience. So, God's spirit is that part of God we can know intimately and vitally. The conclusion of this disclosure is in our receiving and understanding the gifts: "Now we have received . . . the Spirit which is from God, that we might understand the gifts bestowed on us by God" (1 Cor. 2:12).

Spiritual gifts, therefore, are new traits of human character and behavior unknown before our new humanity in Christ (see 2 Cor. 5:17). The gifts do not come through genetic transmission, meditation, or education. They are new abilities whose source is spiritual. Our parents did not inspire or transmit them. Our teachers and coaches did not drill them into our thinking and habits. They are, in Paul's words, *pneumatikon*, "spiritual things" (see 1 Cor. 12:1, 7).

To say that the gifts relate only to the third person of the Trinity is to fall short of Paul's teaching. I believe he deliberately interchanges the words *God, Christ,* and *Holy Spirit* as he speaks of the gifts to show they are of divine origin. The noteworthy passage is 1 Corinthians 12:4-6: "Now there are varieties of gifts [*charismata*], but the same *Spirit* [*pneuma*]; and there are varieties of service [*diakonia*], but the same *Lord* [Christ]; and there are varieties of working [*energemata*], but it is the same *God* who inspires them all in every one" (emphasis mine). "Inspires" here comes from *energon* from which we derive the English word *energy.* Thus, God energizes (endows with power) the new abilities for their operation.

Whether we speak of God, Christ, or Holy Spirit, the gifts are a means of transmitting the powerful and purposeful divine presence into the flesh and blood of humanity. It is an intimacy with God that sheds light on the active presence of the resurrected Christ. It is an inner power that makes the whole person receptive and obedient to a new way of living abundantly and effectively in service to God's kingdom (see John 10:10). In essence, this empowering is a continued incarnation, the fulfillment of our Lord's promises: "He who believes in me will also do the works that I do; and greater works" (John 14:12); and "In that day you will know that I am in my Father, and you in me, and I in you" (John 14:20).

Resources for Operating Spiritual Gifts

Our next concern is the exciting transformation of certain religious activities into resources for the operation of the gifts. I list a sampling of five.

1. **Worship.** The practice of worship becomes more than an inner attitude or a private act. It transcends a passive spectator event to active participation in the very body of Christ. Worship becomes the process of getting in touch with all other members or parts of the same body. The

27

vitality comes from the living Christ whose presence empowers all participants equally with mutual benefits. The motivation for unity and service comes from the dynamic presence of God as Spirit (*pneuma*) who reincarnates the "mind of Christ" in the members of the community of faith (see 1 Cor. 2:16).

The human body is healthy only when all parts and systems work in harmony for mutual benefits. Similarly, the body of Christ in worship is healthy only when all parts (members) as gifts share their energy with and for the benefit of the others. The church at authentic worship requires the presence and operation of all the gifts, not just those operated by the minister and the musicians. When a church is so assembled, no force in the world can withstand its power for good (see Matt. 16:18).

I submit that one way to restore to the church its effectiveness for peace and unity in the affairs of human beings is to discover and use the gifts. I contend further that one way to revitalize what, for many, has become dull and boring rituals of worship is to incorporate understanding, appreciation, and use of the gifts God has bestowed on us.

Medical science defines sickness as a breakdown of communication and transmission of energy between the parts of the human body. It teaches further that nature designs and locates each part to serve the other parts. When any part is dysfunctional, the whole body suffers. The same is true about the church and its various functions.

Instead of predictable rituals, worship becomes an exciting and lasting experience as we use the gifts according to God's will (see Rom. 12:1-2). Worship, therefore, is a coming together of the body parts to celebrate unity of power, position, and purpose. To depart from such an event without a renewed or recharged sense of continuing fellowship in ministry under Christ is to fall short of what true worship offers. The wise leader of worship will want to engage as many gifts as possible.

2. **The Bible.** When we receive and use the gifts for their intended purpose, the Bible becomes more than a sacred paper shrine to be visited now and then. It becomes a living study guide for holy and holistic living. The Bible takes on a new authority, not as a reservoir of unquestioned doctrines, but as a divinely inspired corrective for human error and a cure for apathy and false enthusiasm. The Bible becomes more than a system of beliefs; it is a source of inspired living. Persons who discover their gifts practice a renewed appreciation for and devotion to

scripture. They want to be scriptural in their understanding of God's grace and their special grace-gifts so as not to abuse or neglect them.

3. **Prayer.** Another dimension of an elevated recognition and use of gifts is an attraction to a deeper prayer life, especially using praise and thanksgiving in prayer. Gift consciousness often delivers many persons from predominantly asking God for things to giving praise and thanksgiving. Much of their praying is for guidance to use the gifts in humility and gratitude.

Praying also becomes more than a formalized ritual or mindless habit. It is a constant awareness of God that makes possible an active, two-way communion at all times. Ritual and form in praying are not precluded. In fact, they take on a new symbolic meaning. A good example is the prayer posture. Kneeling and bowing symbolize humility and death. Rising with head up and arms lifted symbolize the blossoming of new life and vigor. As Christians get closer to an understanding and appreciation of their charismatic nature (their giftedness), praying often becomes more open and animated.

4. **Witnessing.** Using one's gifts is more than obedient industriousness. It is a form of witnessing to the grace of God. When persons realize that God has designed and given them special abilities for the general health and ministry of the body of Christ, they become joyfully motivated to share freely with others. Their witness is not the classical and manipulating buttonholing-people-for-Christ, however; it is a careful and deliberate attempt to be open always to the direction of the Spirit and sensitive to the needs of others. This openness teaches us that witnessing has many forms.

Witnessing may be the activity of serving others with our gifts. Charismatic witnessing is not saying, "Look what God has done for me!" (see Rom. 12:3) but looking for opportunities to use our gifts and letting others use theirs. The greatest witness is the health one brings to the body, and that cannot be done by remaining in isolation or by keeping one's gifts a secret. The essence of witnessing is love (*agape*), and love is always something one does, whether in word or in work, for others.

5. **Power.** Although gifted persons want to do everything they can to develop their gifts for full effectiveness, they learn quickly that the essential power comes from God. Knowing and doing God's will are impossible without God's power that accompanies the faithful use of

gifts. It is possible for us to be all that we can be without any direct or conscious reliance on God. It is impossible for us to be *more* than we are without God's presence and power. Spiritual gifts make us extraordinary.

Human nature, despite human efforts to purify and perfect it, is under a curse beyond human control. Paul named the source of this curse "principalities and powers," meaning evil forces. The manifest presence of the Spirit or "spirituals" (see 1 Cor. 12:1) in the new life provided for Christians brings a power (*dunamis*) to overcome certain aspects of the evil forces. This power undergirds the new abilities we know as gifts. These abilities, or *charismata*, counteract the evil powers threatening to destroy all good. The power in any gift, apart from the whole body or interaction of all gifts, is not enough to repel the evil forces. With all members realizing and using their gifts for the common good (see 1 Cor. 12:7), no powers of evil or "gates of hell" can withstand the whole body's force for good (see Matt. 16:18). Evil's power triumphs only when Christians ignore or refuse to use their spiritual gifts for upbuilding the church.

The primary source of spiritual gifts is God who creates a special relationship between the faithful members of the body of Christ. The basis for this special relationship is the common good. Once these abilities, as spiritual gifts, are acknowledged and properly used, certain basic religious activities become powerful resources for aiding the church to fulfill its divine purpose. Some of these activities are worship, Bible study, prayer, and witnessing by word and deed. With the empowerment from the dynamic presence of God's Holy Spirit, they bring about justice and righteousness.

3

What the Spiritual Gifts Are Not

To clear up some misunderstandings about the gifts, I will first describe what the gifts *are not* before looking at what they *are*. To know some things fully and adequately, it is just as important to know what they are not as it is to know what they are. Marriage is a good illustration.

I have been married long enough to have learned some things. It is just as important to know what my wife does not like as it is to know what she does. It's no pleasurable thing, mind you, to hear criticism. But I learned that if I want a meaningful and harmonious relationship, I'd better know what not to bring into our marriage.

Likewise, knowing what not to expect or do as Christians is vital to Christian living. That's why we study the Bible, go to church school, attend seminars, read books, listen to sermons, and share with others. Let's apply this idea to our study of gifts.

First of all, we must understand the word *gift*. Unfortunately, in translating the case from Greek to English, particularly from New Testament Greek (*Koine*) to modern English, some things get lost.

Several Greek words are translated in English as "gift," and all carry nuances and shades of difference in meaning. A list of eight includes *dorea, doma, dosis, dorema, doron, pneumatikon, charis,* and *charisma*.

Each describes an extraordinary blessing God bestows, but the transaction for each seems to carry different reasons or purposes. For instance, *dorea* is a divine favor without a cause. God gives because the nature of divine love is to give. We do not earn or deserve it. It is what we perceive as a part of *agape* love. This love gives and gives and keeps on giving. *Dorea* is used in the phrases "gift of life," "gift of the Spirit," and "gift of righteousness" (see Acts 2:38; 8:20; 10:45; 11:17; Rom. 3:24, 5:17).

When "gift" in an English version of the New Testament has the Greek word *dorea* behind it, the passage describes a blessing God initiates from divine nature to give, not from our merit or need. The gift gives birth to the need, not the opposite. This kind of gift is *not* the subject of this book.

"Gift" translated from *doma* usually involves a legal transaction, a quid pro quo, or something for something. Let me illustrate. A portion of Ephesians 4:8 is not understandable without looking at Psalm 68:18. According to ancient custom, when a warrior succeeded in war, protocol demanded that the captives bring gifts to the new ruler:

> Thou didst ascend the high mount,
>   leading captives in thy train,
>   and *receiving gifts among men.*
>   —Psalm 68:18, emphasis mine

The psalmist used the social protocol as a model for subordination to God. In the Book of Ephesians, our Lord reversed this idea. When he became our captor, out of his liberating (not enslaving) love *"he gave gifts to men"* (Eph. 4:8, emphasis mine). Because he liberates and claims us as captives, he gives gifts to us. In a sense, this concept is very close to *dorea* in that the captives receive something they did not earn or deserve. You see, they lost the contest! Yet, in another sense, *doma* is different from *dorea*. There is a cause—our captivity.

A third significant Greek word that translates as "gift" in English is *pneumatikon* (see 1 Cor. 12:1; 14:1). Some versions (e.g. RSV) translate this as "spiritual gifts" and "gifts of the Spirit." Without getting into a lengthy exegesis to clear up 1 Corinthians 12:2-3, let's focus on Paul's main objective. He is introducing the fact that giftedness (beginning with v. 4) has no worldly or physical origin. He even writes that "no one can say 'Jesus is Lord' except by the Holy Spirit" (verse 3). Actually, 1 Corinthians 12:1 should translate *pneumatikon* as "spirituals" or "spiritual things." Some translations do this. So when you read "gift" in English and discover that it comes from *pneumatikon*, the author is attempting to describe a powerful ability that cannot be worked or psyched up by human effort. It comes from a strictly spiritual source. The root word is *pneuma*, Greek for "Spirit."

The only word we will look at here is the subject and essence of this book, *charisma*. Unlike all the other words that translate from Greek to English as "gift," *charisma* indicates a gift bestowed for a reason. It is a gift that must be used. It is a divinely designed and deliberately distributed ability to be used in building up the body of Christ. It has contingencies and conditions attached; its purpose is service.

Charisma or *charismata*, therefore, carries the key to unlock the church's power and effectiveness as God's instrument for the world's redemption (see 2 Cor. 5:16-19). To gain a fuller understanding of these gifts we must continue our analysis of what the gifts are not.

Spiritual Gifts Are Not Acquired Skills or Natural Talents

The New Testament's use of so many words that translate as "gift" strongly suggests the writers knew that God had given them extraordinary, supernatural abilities. Paul stated, "From now on, therefore, we regard no one from a human point of view" (2 Cor. 5:16). Then he described the "new creation" or new humanity in Christ.

If the spiritual gifts are merely skills or natural abilities, we must admit that someone has played a trick on us. Don't we recognize acquired skills and natural abilities among nonbelievers, even atheists? Sometimes, I must confess, I discover greater skills and abilities among atheists than among believers. Christians do not have the franchise on physical, mental, academic, and social skills.

However, a biblical truth and basic theological principle of Christian faith is that every aspect of life is a gift from God. Many teachers of the Christian faith taught this, and we believe it. But *charisma* or *charismata* is something more.

It is a new dimension to life known and experienced beyond natural abilities. Paul referred to it as "what the eye does not see, the ear does not hear, and the mind cannot imagine, God prepares and reveals to us through the Spirit" (1 Cor. 2:9-10, AP). In reality, this new dimension is more than a gift *from* God. It is God *as* God's gift. The spiritual gift becomes a manifestation of the energizing and empowering presence of God's gift of God (see 1 Cor. 12:7).

REDISCOVERING OUR SPIRITUAL GIFTS

Earlier, Paul said, "Now we have received not the spirit of the world, but the Spirit which is from God, that we might understand the gifts bestowed on us by God" (1 Cor. 2:12). Gifts, therefore, cannot be received or comprehended apart from God who is the giver of the Holy Spirit, which is an expression of God we can experience vividly and intimately.

We are not without problems here. I believe the church is having a severe struggle because we rely mainly on natural interests and skills for which we have no spiritual affinity. The biblical idea of charismatism has a spiritual—nonphysical—attribute that other physical and mental traits do not have. Simply because a person appears to have, or actually displays, an unusual physical or mental adroitness does not mean that he or she has the spiritual power necessary for building up the body of Christ.

Church leaders often search for persons with special training or expertise to fill positions of service in the church. They rarely consider searching for recognizable spiritual affinities, a calling of God, or spiritual gifts (see Rom. 11:29). On the surface, it may appear that suggesting any other way of choosing people for service would be leadership insanity. The sad reality is that we organize and staff most churches without regard for spiritual gifts as God's design for ministry.

Don't we seek persons who work as professionals in finances to manage the local church's money matters? Don't we exult in the discovery of a prospective member who is a public school teacher because we are always in need of teachers? We find a person with manual skills in secular work to put to work doing similar services around the church. We attempt to relate persons to positions in the church according to natural abilities, skills, and secular occupations, but at the risk of losing spiritual genuineness and effectiveness! Is it any wonder why so many of them burn out and the church grows stale?

Paul clearly offers an alternative. In 1 Corinthians 12:7-11 he explains that God gives special abilities (*charismata*) for specific needs in the body of Christ, all according to God's will and not according to our management skills.

God does not overlook natural abilities and training. To the contrary, the talent or trained skill is a means for the operation of a spiritual gift. Think of it in terms of a pipe and water. The pipe is the talent or skill, and the water is the gift that flows through it. God uses natural and developed abilities to transport spiritual gifts. They are intimately and interdependently connected, but not the same.

Consider the person standing in front of a classroom. We call that person a teacher, using the jargon of secular education as a model. Yet, the "teacher" may be doing something other than transmitting or communicating information; that person may be encouraging, inspiring, helping, counseling, or witnessing.

Many people shy away from teaching or refuse to teach, and rightly so, because they do not discern in themselves a spiritual affinity for teaching. Consequently, we often dump guilt on them if they refuse to teach, especially if they have the training and teach in a secular system. To be biblically correct, we should call the setting a fellowship or a sharing, witnessing, discipling, or Bible reading group. Various other spiritual gifts would also be suited for these settings.

Some persons complain about the difficulty of church school curriculum. The problem may be that the secular model for teaching, not spiritual life, is the guide for developing the materials. Many writers of our literature give little, if any, attention to potential users who do not have the spiritual gift of teaching (*didaskalia*) but do have other gifts just as essential for sharing. I dream of a day when publishers will seek persons with specific spiritual gifts to develop materials for others who have the same gifts.

Another significant point relates to the dramatic and devastating decline in church school enrollment and attendance. Obviously, most of what we do isn't working. Yet, we continue to shuttle persons into classes for learning experiences, while their needs may not be education at all. It is possible that they need pastoring, encouraging, or counseling. They may need healing, mercy, or helps. Or what about fellowship or worship? These are different from teaching. This may be the reason teachers whose spiritual gift is not teaching (*didaskalia*) find most of the teaching materials foreign and unfulfilling. The students of the class who are not there to be taught or trained are even more frustrated. The frustration and the resulting inattention discourage the so-called teacher. The conclusion is reduced motivation to teach or attend.

Because the Book of Ephesians identifies one gift as teaching (see Eph. 4:11), we infer that there is a need for that gift's offering. However, other gifts serve some needs that teaching cannot fulfill. Although everyone needs to be taught, we ought not allow anyone to be involved in this ministry who does not have the gift for teaching. Developing the Christian character is just that serious!

God makes no mistakes in the assignments of gifts (see 1 Cor. 12:11). Therefore, we ought to discover them and put them to proper use. Natural abilities or trained skills must never be substitutes for spiritual gifts.

Spiritual Gifts Are Not Roles

In general, some ministries are common and available to all members of the body of Christ. I call them roles. For example, all are witnesses. Jesus said, "You shall be my witnesses" (Acts 1:8). Although our Lord spoke to his immediate disciples, I take it that this imperative reaches us today, for he included "to the end of the earth." Paul lifts up the necessity for witnessing as a means to impart grace to others: "Let no evil talk come out of your mouths, but only such as is good for edifying, as fits the occasion, that it may impart grace to those who hear" (Eph. 4:29).

This type of witnessing is not a manipulative attempt to convert others. It is to share with others our gratitude for God's goodness. Such a witness that praises God imparts God's grace to others. This general witness is the blessed privilege of believers—a role, if you will.

Yet, on a different level, a special, articulate gift brings others to repentance and conversion. It is the spiritual gift of evangelism. It is not a role or general office to which anyone may be appointed. It is a specialized power of God that energizes a divinely selected few who, when they are faithful in their witnessing, specifically and effectively bring others to Christ to receive his redeeming grace. The general witness and the verbal activity of the evangelist gift may sound and appear to be identical, but the difference is in the results. I will say more about this later.

Another example of the difference between role and gift is giving. Every member of the church has the privilege and duty of contributing money to the church's ministries. The Bible teaches tithing and exempts no one from it. But God gives the gift of giving or liberality to certain persons to make money to give money to the church. One test of this gift is that usually the more money these persons willingly give, the more

God blesses them with the power to make more. It is not the other way around.

A couple in a church I served felt inspired by God to supply the pastor with a large amount of money for discretionary purposes. They couldn't have cared less about what happened to the money, though they wanted it to help needy persons. Their contributions were not limited to my church; they gave to many others as well. Obviously, they were not in the business of making money for themselves. Their lack of interest in details of distribution made it clear that they did not have the gift of administration. One of them said to me when I sought advice, "Pastor, you are not to worry us with the details. Our ministry is to provide you with funds to meet needs. If you can't handle this, we'll give the money to another who can. When you need money, come to us. What you do with it, go to God!"

You will never know if you have the gift of giving until you exceed your tithe. Go beyond the biblical imperative to tithe and see what God has in store for you. If you have the gift of liberality, you will know it by the power to fulfill it.

A final illustration is prayer. Hardly anyone questions the universal need to pray, which is a general characteristic of Christians. Beyond this is a special gift of intercessory prayer God gives to certain persons for specific prayer ministries. I will describe it more fully in a subsequent chapter. All are privileged to pray and must pray for the sake of spiritual health, but God gives the gift of intercessory prayer to some.

Spiritual Gifts Are Not Offices

An office in nearly every denomination carries the title of pastor. This office may not have anything to do with the spiritual gift by the same name found in Ephesians 4:11. I have met hundreds of ordained cler-gypersons who hold the office of pastor but who do not have or claim the spiritual gift of pastoring. In contrast, I have met hundreds of laypersons who do have the gift. God does not always follow our institutionalized procedure for ordination. Many laypersons, perhaps more than clergy, are the divinely appointed pastors in local congregations. The office does not automatically guarantee the extraordinary power of the Spirit that energizes the gift.

In the earliest Christian communities there is evidence that without rank and status, even education (see Acts 4:13), certain persons surfaced with extraordinary abilities and insights for the church's development. Paul described this phenomenon as grace for edifying and building up the fellowship. The persons had no titles, since organization was not the purpose of their work.

The nearest Paul came to labeling them was to call them fellow workers and laborers (see 1 Cor. 16:16; 1 Thess. 5:12-13). Paul's fellow workers and laborers were charismatic in that the Holy Spirit filled, motivated, and equipped them for service. Eventually, because of certain peculiarities and needs, descriptive terms came into use to identify the ministries: *pastors, teachers, evangelists, apostles, presbyters, deacons, elders,* and *bishops.* But the next generation brought radical changes.

By the end of the first century, ministries became a community possession. For eighteen centuries the organized church controlled the gifts and managed all ministries. In all branches of the Christian church today, offices and orders for official and professional ministries abound. We can be sure that they are little kin to those initiated and maintained by the energizing presence of God's spirit.

Some ordained ministers today have discovered the difference between their office or order and the biblical notion of charismatic pastoring. Many of them have completely given themselves over to the notion that the church, as an institution, possesses and dispenses the gifts for ministry according to a committee's perfected procedures for selecting candidates, training, ordaining, and appointing. And as a result, a critical problem has developed.

We all know ordained and certified leaders whose personalities, abilities, and effectiveness fall short of authentic manifestations of the Holy Spirit, of which Paul speaks in 1 Corinthians 12. We all know teachers, presbyters, deacons, pastors, bishops, leaders, and administrators whose lives do not exemplify a state of being in Christ or, for that matter, for Christ. We know others who do not hold any official title or certification as ministers but who have unquestionable spiritual power in their caring and sharing as Christians.

Once we get beyond the Bible and into the eighteen centuries of ministries of organized religion, we encounter a profusion of uncertainties over orders. Some denominations today cannot make up their minds about who and what is a minister. I find it difficult to believe that some of our officials and their offices have much to do with God, especially in light of Paul's injunctions: "I bid every one among you not to think of himself more highly than he ought to think . . . love one another with brotherly affection; outdo one another in showing honor . . . never be conceited" (Rom. 12:3, 10, 16); and "Do nothing from selfishness or conceit, but in humility count others better than yourselves" (Phil. 2:3).

It is imperative for us to reintroduce ministries after the example of our Lord to be lived out in unselfish dedication, compassion, and spiritually directed service. I do not suggest that we disassemble our institutionally designed and perpetuated orders and offices. I do recommend, though, a thorough education about the graces and gifts of God that are genuinely and powerfully present in the unofficial and unordained. Learning the difference between God's gifting and human ordering is vital.

Spiritual Gifts Are Not the Fruit of the Spirit

The most common mistake is to identify the fruit and the gifts of the Spirit as the same. We came to this error honestly. My research of the great Christian thinkers and teachers in history discloses similar misunderstandings. Augustine, Aquinas, Calvin, Luther, and John Wesley—to name only a few—show confusion in this area.

Galatians 5:22-23 lists the fruit of the Spirit: "love, joy, peace, patience, kindness, goodness, faithfulness, gentleness, self-control," nine in number. Gifts and fruit are different but connect in the Spirit.

Many commentaries identify "fruit," singular in Greek, as "love" in the Galatian list. The following eight are dimensions or virtues of love. Because of the richness of "love" in Greek, *agape*, especially Paul's use of that word, and because of its profound ramifications for spiritual gifts, "fruit" and "gift" bump into each other, and perhaps overlap, in our thinking and conversations. The distinction should be made clear.

Without question, the attributes or virtues listed after love in Galatians 5:22-23 could not survive without *agape*. We could go further and suggest that the eight others are seeds nurtured by the fruit of love. Each seed carries peculiar and distinguishable characteristics that have a common source of power, which is love. Paul's treatment of love (*agape*) as he explains spiritual gifts is similar. After listing and explaining the gifts, he points to "a more excellent way," which is love (see 1 Cor. 13). All gifts differ markedly, but none is effective without love. That is their common source of power, as it is with the fruit in Galatians 5:22-23.

Although there is no variation in the power of *agape* love, there is a difference between manifestations of that love as fruit or gifts.

The fruit of the Spirit are what we *are*. We have no choice about bearing all the fruit or living out the virtues. Our new spiritual nature as Christians is to be loving through the attributes of joy, peace, patience, kindness, goodness, faithfulness, gentleness, and self-control. We cannot choose between the fruit we want and do not want to produce. The nature of our new humanity in Christ is to bear all the fruit.

The gifts of the Spirit are what we *do*. We have a choice in their operation. We choose to receive and to use the gifts, although we do not choose them. Using the gifts for their intended purposes is essential to the maintenance of one's faith venture. The employment of the gifts is a deliberate act of will. The fruit are the automatic result of love. Gifts are not. Though they have the same root source, *agape* love, they are not the same thing. Gifts can be operated without love—but only as a liability to the body of Christ. The energizing and powerful operation of love that comes from God's spirit is vital to the effectiveness of the employed gift.

Spiritual Gifts Are Not for Self-Gain

We can prove the possibility of having and using the gifts without love through Paul's discourse on gifts in 1 Corinthians 12–14 given in the eye of a hurricane of anarchy and conflict. Persons endowed with special abilities and power to minister elevated themselves and the importance of their gifts over others. Members of the Corinthian congregation drew invidious distinctions between themselves and others, claiming superiority for their particular gifts.

Paul sought to resolve this conflict by setting the gifts in the proper context. They cannot be effectively operated without *agape* love and must never serve selfish ends. To encourage the proper use, he correlated the unity of gifts in the Holy Spirit with the unity we have in the body of Christ. It is good, he explained, to get excited over spiritual gifts, but spiritual pride and arrogance destroy their divine purpose (see 1 Cor.

12:1-3). Gifts misused for selfish gain and spiritual pride become the worst enemies of Christ's church.

Paul's advice in 1 Corinthians 12–14 often remains unheeded. Beginning with the Montanists in the second century, certain pneumatics in the church were all too eager to lord it over others by proclaiming their preeminence. The pattern continued throughout history among other groups: Enthusiasts in Germany, Pietists in England, Pentecostals in America and, most recently, some charismatics. Believing one is superior to other Christians is a terrible sin. Paul admonished the Romans and Corinthians that it is all right to be different: "Having gifts that differ" (Rom. 12:6), and "Now there are varieties of gifts" (1 Cor. 12:4). We have yet to learn this lesson. But it is not all right to value one's gifts as better or superior to others' gifts.

Many persons tarnish the idea and practice of the gifts of speaking in tongues, divine healing, prophecy, and discernment with extreme and bizarre claims and behavior. Because of them, others discount the authenticity and value of the gifts. So, two opinions emerge: that of pneumaphobics, persons who are afraid to have anything to do with the Holy Spirit; and that of pneumanics, those who worship the experience or the gifts and not the Giver. Both hurl unloving accusations at each other, rarely understand each other, and confuse the silent majority between them. One wonders which sin is greater—gift pride, looking down on others with different gifts, or gift denial, not believing in gifts at all.

Paul presents a profound message. The gifts are not limited to a few special members with special rank, but for the common good of the whole church. Common sense tells us that each part of the body is to serve the other parts. The head cannot scratch itself; hands and fingers do that. Ears cannot see, and eyes cannot hear. A tongue cannot kick, and toes cannot taste. The heart cannot think, and the head cannot pump blood. The same is true of the spiritual gifts. My gifts are to serve others, and their gifts are to serve me.

Spiritual Gifts Are Not Divisive

Strife and conflict have flared over the gifts. Most of us know of fits of anger and even congregational splits because of claims, uses, denials, and abuses of gifts. That is a sad commentary on people who should know and want better.

Throughout our history, many Christians have been divided over too much or too little devotion to a good thing. In both cases, God's will and divine causes are the casualties. When these divisions happen, we dare not blame them on God's spirit. God unites, but evil divides.

When a congregation becomes divided over the use of spiritual gifts, someone is sinning. It is not the nature of the Spirit to injure the body of Christ or any of its members in any way. The vital dynamic of the Spirit's presence is always to bring unity, oneness of purpose, singleness of goal—the common good. The edification (health and wholeness) of the church is the strategic test of authenticity for each gift. An unhealthy body cannot produce healthy fruit. Only a healthy body can bear the fruit of righteousness and holiness (see Matt. 7:15-20).

Spiritual Gifts Are Not the Same for Everyone

The biblical passages touching on gifts (*charismata*) offer no hint that any person has all the available gifts or that any of the gifts is for every person. Also, nothing supports an indifferent attitude toward the gifts. We are not free to go our own way without the aid of the gifts.

Although gifts are given to individuals, they flourish with legitimacy and effectiveness in community and for the sake of the whole body of Christ. Paul's theme in 1 Corinthians 12 is multiformity, not uniformity. He works the human body metaphorically to describe the individual members who make up the body of Christ, the church: "To one is given . . . to another . . . to another . . . to another." The gifts are for every member of the body, but no member has them all.

To accept the gifts of the Spirit is not to commit oneself to be a fax copy of every other Spirit-filled Christian. No, as each part of the human body is unique with peculiar characteristics for service, God gives us individuality and uniqueness. Upon receiving a gift or gifts, one does not have to alter behavior, dress, and speech to be spiritual.

The only legitimate conformity, the only common property, related to the gifts is openness and obedience to the Giver of gifts. The only uniformity worthy of acceptance is to be in common subjection to the same Spirit, the same Lord, and the same God. The "varieties of gifts," the "varieties of service," and the "varieties of working" (1 Cor. 12:4-6) are joyous occasions to celebrate God in and through all things.

4

What the Spiritual Gifts Are

We have considered what the gifts are not; now let's explore exactly what these manifestations of the Holy Spirit are.

Spiritual Gifts Are Unmerited Blessings from God

The rich word *grace* is God's unmerited love given by divine initiation and approbation. By unmerited I mean unearned, something we do not deserve. Grace cannot be obtained through human effort. God's grace is free and full. Yet, unmerited grace does not mean unneeded grace. We need God's love desperately. God's grace is essential for our salvation, our wholeness and fulfillment. So God loves us not only because it is divine nature to do so but also because of our great need. We can know this love as saving grace and serving grace. Saving grace is the same for everyone; serving grace is different from one person to another.

Charismata (gifts) come into the relationship at this point. They are special powers and abilities given to build the body of Christ, the church. They are also for the fulfillment of the wholeness of each member.

The similarity in all the gifts is that God chooses them and the persons to receive them (see 1 Cor. 12:11). By definition, a gift is not a gift if it can be earned or appropriated by the receiver. The *charisma* is something freely given and freely received, and God is the giver.

The psychological and social blessings that accompany God's assignment of a gift are threefold. First, the grateful recipients become motivated to do everything possible with their gifts as an expression of gratitude in faithful service for God. Second, in fulfilling their gifts' potential and purpose, recipients never consider themselves in competition with other members of the body of Christ. They are not envious or jealous of others with different gifts (see 1 Cor. 13:4-5). Third, faithful operation of the gifts brings such joy and power that the recipients never burn out. They may wear out but will never burn out.

Spiritual Gifts Are Job Descriptions for Ministries

Because of our fallen and sinful nature, we could never design an effective method of recovery and health (salvation). God has accomplished salvation for us through Jesus Christ. Our Lord created the church and made it his continued agent of divine healing for others. The members enjoy a fellowship sustained and empowered by the presence of the resurrected Christ. Still, there is more to the Christian life than merely to be saved and to enjoy the fellowship of Christ and other Christians. The church is an instrument by which the entire world may be made whole (see 2 Cor. 5:18-20).

The spiritual gifts are special ministries distributed throughout the membership of the church for power and success in mission to itself (for health and vitality) and, through itself, to the world (redemption). The spiritual gifts are the functional requisites for a fully operational force to bring about wholeness, righteousness, and justice. They are job descriptions for an every-member ministry.

Without the presence and proper employment of gifts, the church is no more than any other group trying to do good things. Unlike other groups, when the church does not acknowledge and faithfully use the gifts, its fellowship becomes flat and full of crippling conflicts.

Many church leaders see today's mounting conflicts heading toward a repeat of the first-century crises. Many local churches are learning what it is to be "tossed to and fro and carried about with every wind of doctrine" (Eph. 4:14) as they try desperately to stay afloat. Their long history of growth, influence, and prestige is eroding rapidly. To offset this threat of ineptitude and tension, the church must discover and use the power in its gifts.

God's design for health, vigor, unity, purpose, and success is the every-member ministry based on gifts given "to equip the saints for the work of ministry for building up the body of Christ" (Eph. 4:12). Today's church, threatened by decline and extinction, would do well to rediscover the New Testament model for service—the gifts. Receiving God's gifts and using them for ministry and mission is our greatest hope for a healthy church.

Spiritual Gifts Are a Means for Discovering God's Will

Can you think of anything more joyous and meaningful than discovering God's will for your life? Paul says that the purpose of our gifts is to "prove what is the will of God, what is good and acceptable and perfect" (Rom. 12:2). He is so carried away with the thoughts of God's will that in the midst of a discourse on Israel's history, he pauses to shout for joy. He proclaims,

> O the depth of the riches and wisdom and knowledge of God! How unsearchable are his judgments and how inscrutable his ways! . . . For from him and through him and to him are all things. To him be glory for ever. Amen.
>
> —Romans 11:33, 36

Then Paul reminds us of the privilege of making every sacrifice to know the mind and will of God. Nothing gives Christians more pleasure than discovering God's will. Also, nothing is more confusing and disheartening than attempting to serve without God's will, calling, and empowerment (see Rom. 11:29).

Not to know God's will is spiritual immaturity (see Heb. 5:11-14). To know God's will is to be liberated for new life and direction. This liberation also frees us from feelings of guilt often experienced when we do not or cannot do something God has not called or equipped us to do.

In my workshops on spiritual gifts, many persons find joyful release from some guilt feelings. They discover that it is OK not to minister (or want to) in ways they are not called or gifted. Many, for example, carry guilt over hesitating to teach when asked. They admit that other services are far more appealing and that they would respond favorably if asked to do them. Yet, the church asks them to do a service that does not give them the sense of God's will or favor. Often, their motivation to serve comes from guilt, coercion, or the fear of being accused of being unfaithful. Some do not feel good enough about themselves to volunteer

45

for something else more in line with what they perceive as God's will. But when others discover that they do not have the gift for a particular service, they experience a joyful freedom to explore other possibilities.

I have seen ordained ministers burst into sudden joy over discovering why they felt so dark and joyless while doing some ministries expected of them. They did not have the gifts for them. When they realized that certain chores are merely roles expected of them as employees, they felt that it was OK not to be blissful about them. They were delivered from guilt over not enjoying those roles and performed the necessary chores with greater ease and less resistance.

Discovering God's will does not relieve a person from assuming reasonable responsibilities in other areas of service where no one is fulfilling them. Most of us can identify things that bring no pleasure at all but must be done. The office of pastor requires some activities that offer no immediate delight. Yet, the person who knows God's will and gift understands that nothing is futile or senseless that relates to the body of Christ. Although some things are not pleasurable, they may be essential. To do the essential with a proper attitude is to experience enough of God's grace to make it meaningful. To discover one's gifts for ministry is also to discover God's will for unity and purpose in all forms of serving.

Spiritual Gifts Are Guarantees of Effective Service

A person sick or weakened by age is rarely that way because the whole body is ill. It takes only one or two parts of the body to stop functioning properly. A breakdown in communication or energy flow between organs and systems of the human body can critically reduce the performance of the whole body.

The same is true for the church, the body of Christ. When any member fails to use or rejects God's gifts for body life, the whole body suffers. Ephesians 4:16 emphasizes that when each part of the body is working properly, the body grows and is built up in love.

I have worked with hundreds of churches, some of which were healthy and vital and others tragically sick. Some constantly engaged in high voltage programs and high octane activity; many more remained sadly passive. Yet, I have come to realize that programs and activity alone cannot maintain health enough for survival any more than eating and exercise alone can sustain the human body.

Sometimes, the body needs to stop, take a rest, sleep, and dream. At other times, it needs to take a vacation. Then there are times when the body needs strenuous exercise. But always and everywhere, health and growth require all parts to function fully and properly.

Congregational vitality requires the application of the same principle. To be effective, we must find the proper place to do God's will. We need to recognize other members' place and the value of their gifts. Effectiveness in sustaining fellowship and outreach ministries comes from all gifts working together in mutual interdependance.

Spiritual Gifts Are a Means to Efficient Service

This point may appear similar to the previous one, but it is different. By efficient I mean knowing what, when, and where to do the right thing. We can do the right thing at the wrong time. We can have the right people in the wrong places. I have discovered this problem in too many churches, even pulpits! Time is an apt illustration.

Considerable research shows why churches grow or decline. For nearly two thousand years, until the mid-1960s, most churches automatically grew. Then a dramatic decline began, which has not bottomed out, but we have learned much from studying the trend.

One discovery surprised most clergypersons. The ordained or professional minister thinks about the church twenty-four hours per day, in every place and situation. Hardly one wakes up during the night or lives through a single hour of the day without thinking church. Unfortunately, ministers assume that laypersons do the same thing. A national poll indicated that laypersons give very little thought to the church during the day, and none reported any thought of it when awakened at night. We have also learned that we cannot expect from laypersons more than eight hours per week given in direct service to the church. These eight hours per week include church school and worship. I have asked hundreds of laypersons, "Whenever you wake up in the early hours of the morning, say, two or three o'clock, do you ever think church?" No one has given me a yes answer to that. Very few respond affirmatively when I ask about their frequent thoughts during the course of the day. Isn't it a fact that if people do not "think" church, they are not likely to "do" church?

Isn't it reasonable, then, to find ways to gain the greatest benefit from our members by using their available time where they are the most gifted? The discovered and acknowledged spiritual gift is the place to begin.

To be sure, some people think that although they may not be physically present, they are nonetheless working and doing their part elsewhere. Maybe, but can the body survive with the heart in one place and the spleen and the bladder somewhere else? Many members excuse their absence and contend that they can be independent representatives of the gospel in the world "where it really counts." They deny an integral aspect of the divine nature of the church, which is *koinonia* (fellowship). The spirit of God creates this fellowship only through physical, spiritual, social, and psychological contacts. This type of fellowship makes the church different from any other human effort.

While the church has a hiddenness that we do not comprehend, we must never neglect its essential physical unity and visibility. We often hear about the universal church. Some even excuse their lack of local participation with their claim of being a part of something greater. The fact is that the universal church does not exist without the local, concrete, and visible mixing of caring and sharing members.

A church member's love and compassion shown at secular work may have little or nothing to do with the spiritual gifts. The gifts are for nurturing and maturing the body of believers. The believers need to be physically present to participate in that unity.

If it is a fact that members have only eight hours per week to give directly to the fellowship, we must do everything possible to help them serve fully out of their gifts. We must endeavor to achieve what I call efficiency in gifts management.

Spiritual Gifts Are Securities for Health and Growth

Using the human body as an analogy to describe the church makes it reasonable to assign some value to health and growth for the local church. Medical science helps us to understand this analogy.

The increases of medical knowledge, practice, and spending cause us to assume that health is important to life. Following this course, most health disciplines consider specialization necessary for artful therapy and healing and for preventing illness. Each specialization is born out of the discovery of the essential value of each body part (organ or system) for the good of the whole. The principle is that health depends on the proper and full functioning of every part, which is a legitimate analogy for understanding the church's health and growth.

Each member of the church ought to be physically and spiritually healthy. The spiritual gifts of healing are given for this reason (see 1 Cor. 12:9, 28). These gifts (notice the plural) of healing cover physical, mental, social, financial, and spiritual health. Health can be helped and hindered in many ways. Unfortunately, preoccupation with only physical healings causes us to neglect the other essentials for wholeness.

I have observed this oversight in many churches. A popular practice is calling for audible prayer requests. Then the leader lifts them in the main prayer. This practice is commendable, but I am concerned that almost all requests are for physical healing. I have yet to hear a request for the healing of nations, peace for a troubled family, or deliverance from some emotional illness or attitude. I have heard no one request the healing of the church's ineffectiveness in the midst of mounting evils in the community and world or ask for guidance about halting the decline of its membership in the midst of a growing population. I have never heard anyone request prayer for restoration of financial security or success in finding needed employment.

The local church that discovers its gifts will also find that its health and growth depend on all gifts. Health of body, mind, and soul is essential for effective and productive ministries, and that wholeness and holiness are equated with health and growth.

Spiritual Gifts Are the Revealed Presence of the Living Christ

Paul's analogy of the human body to describe the church's corporate nature is not the whole picture. He also speaks of God's spirit residing in the individual members who make up the body. This truth is one of our big mysteries. The flesh and spirit of each member is the temple of God's dwelling. But all members together are greater than the sum of the parts. The church is more than a mere aggregate of individual members. It is the body of Christ, made alive by the ubiquitous and dynamic spirit of the living Christ. The church, therefore, takes on the personality of Christ as all members interact with love and compassion. When each part (member and gifts) participates fully, the church unmistakably reveals the real presence of Christ (see Eph. 4:11-16).

Spiritual Gifts Are the Guarantor of Lasting Results

Roles and offices for ministries in the church are significant but must never overshadow or supplant gifts (*charismata*) for ministry. Gifts are actual manifestations of the Holy Spirit (see 1 Cor. 12:7) and, thus, guarantee durable results. The inevitable results are "for building up the body of Christ" and opportunities for everyone to "grow up in every way into him who is the head, into Christ" (Eph. 4:12, 15).

Furthermore, the genius of Paul's use of the human body as a metaphor to describe the church also suggests permanency for the gifts. Many people have asked me whether God gives one gift for a particular need or situation and another gift at another time and condition. If we follow the logic in the use of the human anatomy as an analogy, we find our answer.

Aren't we comforted to know that when we get up each morning we can expect the various parts of the body to be where they were when we went to bed? It would be a nightmarish existence not to know from one day to the next or from one situation to another what body parts we can expect to be present and functioning and where!

One of the many joys of receiving God's gifts for ministry is this permanency. We can have the gifts long enough to discover them, develop them, and use them whenever the need arises. When the body of Christ is gathered, we are comforted to know that God has arranged the ministries so that all members may have the full care they need (see 1 Cor. 12:23).

5

Varieties of Gifts, Services, and Results

Paul declared, "Now there are varieties of gifts, but the same Spirit; and there are varieties of service, but the same Lord; and there are varieties of working, but it is the same God who inspires them all in every one" (1 Cor. 12:4-6).

In this chapter, we will examine the gifts' variation, classification, application, and expectations. The main passages are Romans 12:6-8, 27-30; 1 Corinthians 12:8-11; Ephesians 4:6-8; and 1 Peter 4:10-11.

Variation

Romans 12:6-8 lists seven gifts: prophecy, service, teaching, exhortation, giving, leadership, and mercy. The Corinthian text names seventeen in all, but only twelve if we omit repetitions: wisdom, knowledge, faith, healing, miracles, prophecy, discernment, tongues, interpretation, apostle, helps, and administration. The Book of Ephesians (4:11) enumerates five gifts: apostles, prophets, evangelists, pastors, and teachers. First Peter 4:10-11 seems to distinguish two categories of gifted ministries: speaking and serving. When we subtract the repetitions, the total is twenty-one. We need to be careful, though, not to limit the infinite grace of God by holding to that number.

I believe we have not scratched the surface of the broad reaches of God's love through divine gifts. With this in mind, I identify eleven additional New Testament ministries that I consider gifts, which brings my count to thirty-two. Although the gifts not listed in the Bible are possibly rich and wide, I have chosen to confine this discussion to the gifts I believe the scriptures cover.

To be fair, we must understand that there are different schools of thought concerning the identity and number of gifts. My reading of available literature on spirtual gifts turned up five such schools.

1. One says that no gifts exist today, that all *charismata* ceased with the passing of the apostolic age; the gifts were first-century signs of the coming of God's kingdom, useful only then and not now. According to this school, a proper understanding of spiritual gifts or the Holy Spirit, for that matter, requires demythologizing scripture.

2. Another opinion is that only some gifts remain today; the other gifts ended immediately after the birth of the church. The gifts that passed away are the so-called sign gifts, such as miracles, healing, tongues, interpretation of tongues, and prophecy. The sign gifts are no longer needed, the adherents of this school say. The remaining ones are for the maintenance and growth of the church today.

3. A third conviction asserts that though all gifts are still with us, only some persons possess them. The church hierarchy may dispatch or dispense with the operation of any or all gifts according to its corporate wisdom and authority (see Matt. 16:18-19).

4. Others claim that all Christians have all the gifts, and the circumstance determines which gift to use. They support this claim with 1 Corinthians 12:6, "It is the same God who inspires them all in every one." The key to this view is the baptism of the Holy Spirit; the gift of the Holy Spirit brings all spiritual gifts with it.

5. The fifth school, the one with which I identify, maintains that all gifts are just as needed and valid today as they were in the first century. Our belief is that the varieties Paul wrote about in 1 Corinthians 12:4-6 exceed our current comprehension. If there is little or no evidence of certain gifts today, limited faith and spiritual ignorance—and perhaps disobedience—account for the deficiency. Paul addressed this issue in 1 Corinthians 12:1 and warned against it in 1 Thessalonians 5:19.

I refuse to believe we know all there is to know about God and the gifts of the Spirit (see 1 Cor. 2:10). I do not believe the Bible contains all God has to reveal. I believe God is so limitless and all-loving that the abundant life Jesus offers in John 10:10 is far more than we could ever imagine. To discover more is to open ourselves to divine possibilities and spiritual realities (see 1 Cor. 2:9). According to the Gospel of John, Jesus did so much more that "the world itself could not contain the books that would be written" (John 21:25).

This life—here and now, the abundant life (see John 10:10)—is more than a personal or private reality. It is also a sacred, corporate quality we experience in the fellowship with other Christians. It is a body life made up of an infinite variety of grace-events and grace-filled persons. As this grace enters the lives of individual members of the body, their faithful service makes them the means of God's grace.

The operation of gifts (*charismata*) is no less a sacrament than the ritual of the Lord's Supper, or Holy Communion. Don't most Christians believe the elements of bread and wine are the means and symbols of God's grace? Couldn't the sacraments also include the body of Christ whose members God chooses and equips to build one another up with grace-gifts? If bread and wine are sacred means of grace, so is each member of the body of Christ who faithfully uses the grace-gifts (see Rom. 12:1).

In the Lord's Supper, Holy Communion, or Eucharist we believe we encounter something more than mere tokens or reminders of our Lord's broken body and shed blood. It is our Lord's real and effectual presence as the resurrected and living Christ (see Matt. 18:20). Also, in the use of gifts we encounter not merely persons of flesh and blood who receive them, but the presence of Christ who gives them (see 1 Cor. 1:30).

With this in mind, we can see how Paul pushes us to understand grace as limitless. His use of "varieties" for "gifts," "service," and "working" and his careful expansion of divinity with the use of "Spirit," "Lord," and "God" suggest spiritual infinitude (see 1 Cor. 12:4-6). What we know and comprehend is the mere tip of the iceberg. There is much more to learn and to discover. Yet, for our purposes here, we limit our study to the Bible's lists of gifts. I view them as more illustrative than comprehensive.

The central issue here is that all gifts, ways of using them, and their results are of "the same Spirit . . . the same Lord . . . the same God." Do we dare limit the Spirit, Lord, and God to the first century and to 21 or 121 specific demonstrations of grace?

I remember something I read from Cyril of Jerusalem, who wrote, "The same rain comes down upon all the earth, yet it becomes white in the lily, red in the rose, purple in violets and pansies, and different and various in all kinds." We could apply this principle to the sunshine. The same rays of the sun touch all plants equally. The synthesizing process of the rays within the plants is obviously different, but the rays are from the same sun.

This illustration may help us to understand the results of God's grace. The processing and results from one person to another are obviously different—not superior. When we celebrate certain gifts as more important or superior, we lose sight of the divine giver of grace. As rain and sunshine bring a variety of beauty, shapes, sizes, aromas, and fruit in the plants, God's grace (*charis*) brings a variety of beauty, power, and results in the gifts.

Classification

Some people label certain gifts *speaking gifts*. Under this heading, they list exhortation (see Rom. 12:8), utterance of wisdom, utterance of knowledge (see 1 Cor. 12:8), tongues, prophecy (see 1 Cor. 12:10), and teaching (see 1 Cor. 12:28). The problem here is that speaking is not the only means of doing prophecy and teaching.

Others may be classified *serving gifts*. These are administration, helps, leadership, giving, mercy, and service. Aren't all gifts for serving?

A third ordering may be *sign gifts*. Examples are healing, tongues (already listed), interpretation of tongues, miracles, and discernment.

Classifying may be done in many more ways. But I offer a word of caution. It is easy to lose sight of the gifts in rigid categorizing. Let me illustrate.

In 1 Corinthians 12:8, the Greek word *logos* translates as "utterance" in some English versions and "word" in others. Classifying "utterance" as a speaking gift seems acceptable since it is a sound action, done with vocal cords and ears. To "utter" something suggests a speaking-hearing activity. The obvious error is a tendency to overlook the other translations of *logos* into "word." "Word" can be found in more places than just speaking. The essence of Paul's use of *logos* is a means of communication, not a definition.

Many dangers are associated with systems of classification and dispensations for spiritual gifts. Any single method limits our hope of reviewing and renewing the claims of the Holy Spirit on the church in this new day of opportunities. Surely, we need to know much more about God and living by God's will. Perhaps we need to turn to faithful application of what we already know.

Application

Application is a means by which one may execute the calling of God to declare and to promote God's redemption, righteousness, and justice in the affairs of humanity.

The gifts are divine abilities to bring about justice, wholeness, and righteousness, simplified and exemplified in the life and works of Jesus Christ. The ultimate goal of revealing God's glory in all things and persons is the central theme of the four major passages that deal with the gifts. In 1 Corinthians 12:4-6, Paul uses three times the Greek word *diairesis*, which means "many," "varied," or "multiple." I take it that Paul is trying to convince us that the ways to apply the gifts are limitless.

The key Greek word for "application" is *diakonia*, often translated "service" or "ministry." A combination of these two makes it exciting to think how many ways the body of Christ may be ministered to and may be in ministry to others. For example, take the gift of utterance of knowledge (*gnosis*). There is no limit to the possibilities for revealing, delivering, and declaring such knowledge. Speaking with the mouth and writing with the pen are only two ways of doing this. Messages from God may be acted out, painted, sculpted, woven, molded, carved, set to music, and played on musical instruments.

Another example is "wisdom" (*sophia*), which makes room for services and vocations other than religious rituals, such as praying, preaching, and playing hymns on the piano. This gift enables plumbers, electricians, custodians, tailors, police officers, firefighters, nurses, politicians, dentists, druggists, and truck drivers to use their skills in loving and caring service to build up the body of Christ, the church.

Wisdom helps us to transform talents, developed skills, and special interests into grace-filled ministries. Yet talents and gifts are not the same. But the specific spiritual gift of wisdom may be executed or acted out in and through the talents, skills, and natural abilities.

There is no limit to the different ways gifts may be used in serving the

55

church for growth and maturity. For instance, persons with the gift of leadership can serve by dreaming up and creating ways by which the other gifts can be used. Leadership is the power to visualize opportunities and goals that offer health and growth. At heart, the leader is a visionary and dreamer, one who sees connections, directions, and results quickly. The gift of administration, as a contrast, takes over and organizes appropriate gifts and skills to bring the leader's dreams into reality. The administrator knows how to organize and manage others and materials to fulfill dreams that bear God's will.

This process could go on and on, attaining various levels of ministries and broadening scopes of services in the common pursuit of maturing all in Christ (see Eph. 4:13).

Expectations

An encouraging aspect of the gospel is that our gifts and calling do not depend entirely on us. I have already stated that our calling is to be more than what we are and to do more than what we can. This is no riddle or play on words. It is a spiritual reality. On our own, in the flesh, we are hopeless. Who or what we are makes no sense without a divine someone or sacred something in control. Because of who God is and what God does for us in Jesus Christ, we can let our expectations soar to new heights and wonders.

It is tempting to think that we don't count, that even with gifts, whatever they are, we don't amount to much. This thinking overlooks the energizing presence of God's grace in the operation of the gifts. We ought to receive Paul's encouragement in 1 Corinthians 12:6 where he uses "working" and "inspires." Both come from *energma* in Greek, from which we get the English word *energy*. The grace of God is a spiritual energy that has no physical origin, but it affects and empowers the material of our flesh for spiritual and noble purposes. Paul tells us that the gifts we operate really work because God works them (see Phil. 2:13). Because of this spiritual energy or divine grace, faithful use of our gifts is nothing short of miraculous. It goes beyond mere human abilities. The results are manifold and inestimable simply because they become the very energy of God flowing with purpose and freedom.

The heart of each spiritual gift is this energizing grace of God. Grace cannot be earned. It is God's gift of love given by divine choice. We cannot get it on our own. We cannot manipulate it, appropriate it, or manufacture it. It is a gift from God. We either receive it or reject it. If we receive it, it beomes a powerful ability for effective ministry. In the operation of the gift, the grace finds a new outlet and channel to others. The effects in others whom we serve are not our doing; they are the direct results of God's flowing grace. Thus, the results belong to God. The gift is a conduit through which God's grace moves.

We do not have to worry about the results, since they belong to God. Our calling is to discover the spiritual ability and use it for its intended purpose. Nothing in the scheme of God's salvation is more demonstrative of obedient discipleship than our grateful reception of the gifts of the Spirit and our proper use of them.

Because the church can do anything for the betterment of humanity when it is receptive to God's energizing grace, we do not have to worry about the welfare of persons and the world. We can confidently believe God will take care of the needs of the world as we faithfully receive and use our spiritual gifts. More than this, we cannot do; less than this, we dare not do. We have the plan, equipment, and divine empowerment to be the instrument of redemption for the whole human race. The gifts of the Spirit guarantee immediate and lasting results.

6

A Gift Is a Gift Is a Gift Is a Gift

Spiritual gifts are *special, extraordinary abilities God gives to build up the body of Christ, the church, for ministry to its members and, through its members, the world.* God's grace excludes no faithful disciple of Christ. The gifts distinguish between church membership and authentic discipleship. Just because someone is a member of a local church does not mean that the person is a Christian. Also, though a person receives one or more of the gifts, the individual may be unfaithful and thus powerless to operate the gift successfully. Faithful discipleship is necessary for the effective operations of the gifts.

Some manifestations of certain gifts may resemble behavior of natural abilities, but there is a difference in their effect on the body of believers, the church. Also, the authentic effects should be measured for a long period, not just for the immediate time. By testing the gifts in this way, we can determine which gifts are truly spiritual gifts.

We can be certain that Satan attempts to duplicate, if not outdo, anything good that comes from God. The Bible is full of illustrations, and it is no less true today. Let's look at some ways of discerning the true from the false.

One way is to determine if the user of a gift acts for self-gain or recognition instead of loving and caring service for others (see Acts 5:1-11; 8:17-25). If we are not self-seeking or self-serving in our judgment, we can see what is not authentic in some who claim the gift (see 1 Cor. 2:15-16).

Another method of differentiating between true and false gifts is to look at the results. God is not playing a game with us. We play the games, with God and with ourselves. If God's gifts are to build up the body of Christ, the church, they will not divide it or tear it down. Healing will heal, teaching will teach, hospitality will make friends, leadership will gain followers, and evangelism will win new persons to Christ.

Consider these questions to figure out whether gifts are of God or of human want and pride. Is there an attitude of superiority about the presence and use of a particular gift? Paul warns us against this (see Rom. 12:3). Do we ever discount the value of another's gift? Paul cautions against this in 1 Corinthians 12:14-26. Do we believe we have certain gifts because we asked God for them? Paul doesn't teach this in 1 Corinthians 12:11. Are we ever jealous of another's gifts? Read 1 Corinthians 13:4.

The gifts are not private or secret. The whole body must know what and where they are if we are to be healthy. Every member should be interested in and inquisitive about the extraordinary abilities of the other members. So that we can recognize the gifts, let's examine some of their prominent signs.

In this chapter and the next six chapters, I list the gifts in alphabetical order. The scriptural references are given in Gifts' Definitions and Biblical References, page 177. Please keep in mind that these definitions and descriptions of behavioral manifestations do not include the influence of other gifts. That is, each gift has its own peculiarities, as does each part of the human anatomy, but a companion gift may alter it somewhat. What the eyes see can be altered by what the ears hear, and vice versa. What the fingers feel may be altered by what the tongue tastes. So it is with the spiritual gifts. Also, be aware that no two gifts conflict; they always complement each other.

Administration

The word "administration" comes from *kubernesis* in Greek and often describes the position and responsibility of a pilot or helmsman of a ship. It is a directional and managerial ministry.

This *extraordinary ability manifests itself in organizing and coordinating persons and materials effectively to reach objectives and goals consistent with God's plan for the church.*

Though not the owner, the administrator claims responsibility for the successful operation and management of certain ministries. The recipient can view a ministry's full scope, its past, present, and future. This member pursues objectives and plans laid out by the corporate wisdom of the body without acting like a dictator. He or she works out of a strong conviction that if you work the plan, the plan will work.

These gifted persons have an organizational mind that easily and effectively puts people, materials, and schedules into perspective according to a realistic appraisal of goals, resources, and time. Persons with this dominant gift can also easily discern goals, dreams, and plans that are not realistic or workable. They have an insatiable need for clarity of objectives and procedure. They can anticipate the skills and talents necessary to succeed and the problems that can hinder a project.

These gifted persons conserve resources and strictly follow a schedule so that supplies and time do not run out before the project's end. They often hold available resources in reserve at the beginning of a project; this assures them of a means to complete the mission. They often resist explaining why a ministry is necessary and simply tell what is to be done while organizing for successful results. Doing something according to plans and schedule and seeing it through to completion are extremely important. Persons with this gift often appear to be fussy about details and time, but only because they see the total picture of how all things and persons fit together.

The gift of administration focuses predominantly on organization, details, schedule, and skills instead of the persons involved. This focus can be a weakness and potential abuse of the gift. If a person with this gift loses or neglects the relationship with the Holy Spirit, insensitivity to other persons may be the result.

The administrator finds more joy in smooth operations and forward movement than in the actual completion of the project. Activity and involvement are keys to the joy of this gift. Often, after a project's finish, the gifted administrator feels lonely and partial. He or she feels a need to get back into a process.

Facts, practical experience, and necessary details impress administrators. A change in direction, goal, or procedure often frustrates them once the project is under way. They prefer action to conversations about details and avoid hindering persons and circumstances. They are painstakingly thorough. They work hard, carry responsibility especially well, and talk mainly about procedure and quality participation.

A truly inspired administrator was John Wesley, founder of the Methodist movement. While we recognize his other gifts, such as evangelism, wisdom, and teaching, there is no question about his extraordinary ability to organize. Many historians enjoy pointing out the difference between Mr. Wesley and his colleague, George Whitefield, the evangelist. The latter was an effective revival preacher who won hundreds and thousands to Christ, but his ability to organize them was like a "rope of sand." In contrast, John Wesley could take the smallest number of hardly literate and socially uncouth persons and organize them into a solidarity force that will probably last forever.

Persons with this gift often are placed in or seek positions of authority. This way, they can do what they are best at doing—organizing persons, time, and supplies for maximum and lasting benefit. To them, duty is first; preserving and caring follow, in that order.

When others propose goals and projects, administrators ask the hard questions, such as: What is the purpose? Who is going to do it? What's it going to cost? Do you have enough time? Where are we going to get the money? These questions are always sobering, if not disconcerting, for dreamers and visionaries, persons with the gift of leadership.

Paul insists on the presence of love (*agape*) to undergird every gift (see 1 Cor. 13). This word of caution is especially important for administration, since it centers on service and procedure more than persons. The presence of love (*agape*) does not permit this gift, or any other, to get impersonal and insensitive enough to do harm to the body. The gifts are gifts of the Spirit, and the Spirit pours God's love into our hearts (see Rom. 5:5). Love is not without gifts, but gifts without love are demonic. First Corinthians 13 is Paul's warning about irreparable harm that comes from doing good in the wrong way.

Nominating committees should seek persons with this gift to chair various other committees, boards, and projects. A chairperson with this dominant gift offers great hope of not wasting time, energy, supplies, and money on a project. This trait is essential in today's world when most people are already too busy. The church does them no graceful favor by overlooking the need for efficiency in mission.

Apostle

The Greek *apostolos*, which means "ambassador," "delegate," "one sent out," "a messenger," "a herald," is the source of this word. It has two origins. One is a nautical term for a vessel carrying authorized cargo, whether military or commercial. Another origin is political and refers to one who represents another with full power and authority. The word appears seventy-nine times in the New Testament, sixty-eight of which appear in Luke's and Paul's writings. The specific references to a spiritual gift are 1 Corinthians 12:28 and Ephesians 4:11.

The apostle, in a general sense, *forms a strong attachment to the personality, teaching, and influence of Jesus Christ. Then the person spreads the teachings and extols the virtues of that Christ. This apostle of Christ is sent out to bear Christ's authority.*

A contentious question many persons raise is whether we have apostles today. Some say we don't because the gift passed away with the so-called apostolic age. They assert that Christ's first twelve followers were the only apostles.

However, Paul claimed apostleship, and he was not one of those twelve followers (see Rom. 1:1; 1 Cor. 9:1; 2 Cor. 12:12). Likewise, Barnabas was an apostle, yet he was not of those twelve. Furthermore, the New Testament names others as apostles (see Acts 14:14; Rom. 16:7; 1 Thess. 2:6). I see no reason to think that this gift passed away. The church and society need authoritative messengers for Christ today.

Discipleship is a word used a lot today. But there's a difference between discipleship and apostleship. We need both. The apostle has the extraordinary ability to cultivate receptivity toward Christ and Christ's ongoing ministries. Those with other gifts, such as evangelists and teachers, specifically win and disciple persons for Christ. The apostles of Christ are ambassadors, organizers, and cultivators of means for ministries. They are like cargo ships bringing needed supplies for the moment and also like organizers who can put new people in touch with a reliable source to satisfy all their needs.

Some people say that missionaries do the same thing. I view the missionary gift as something different. I will discuss this point in detail later. Briefly, though, missionaries are especially gifted to go beyond

63

culture and languages to do more than win new people to Christ. They go in after the apostles and disciple persons into the wholeness and holiness of kingdom living. Some missionaries may have the gift of apostleship, but not all missionaries are apostles; all apostles are not missionaries. Some missionaries are not gifted messengers or heralds, although they fulfill Christian ministries in various other ways. They teach agriculture, develop technology, practice medicine, construct buildings, houses, and schools, and teach good health practices. Missionaries flesh out Christian love in their varied professions. This is not *apostolos*.

We must not confuse this gift with an office in the church. The New Testament lists certain offices, such as elder, presbyter, bishop, and deacon. Apostle is nowhere included as an office. Paul says it is a spiritual gift; he never declares that *apostolos* can be transmitted from one to another by the laying on of hands. God, not human beings, gives the gift of *apostolos*.

A strong segment of traditionalism elevated some early disciples who obviously had this gift to a special office of authority and rank. From this came the apostolic succession, making all others in the body second-class citizens. This medieval distortion of church life divides the body of Christ between the ordained and the laity, the latter being second rate. The New Testament does not support this division and ranking. Although *apostolos* carries authority and power in its operations, it does not make anyone superior.

When apostles serve as superintendents, program coordinators, or administrators, powerful operations accompany their efforts. They are prone to concentrate more on group activity than on individuals. They have a special spiritual power to get groups of persons moving on the same track toward common goals. They are equally effective among people who know them and those who do not know them.

They have an aura of spiritual authority and power that causes cohesion and unity even among persons who differ widely in attitude and interests. Unlike the gift of administration, which effectively organizes materials and persons, the power of the apostle resides in what he or she reflects and represents, our Lord. The apostle's power is a translucent quality through which the powerful and living Christ moves. Unless we place persons with this gift in our churches' hierarchy, we are not likely to regain the spiritual power we once had to win others to Christ and to build the church.

Positions of rank and authority never create or improve one's ability to be spiritually effective in kingdom living. The dynamically alive and powerful Christ turned loose in the obedient use of the gift of *apostolos* makes the structural ranks and positions worthy as means of God's marvelous grace.

I do not see the gift of apostle as a major ministry in a local church. This gift is a means to go out and unite many local churches under the lordship of Christ who is the head. I do see local persons with this gift as ones who recognize the means and methods of cooperative ministries. They easily inspire their sisters and brothers to reach out to others for cooperative efforts to obey and minister for Christ as head over all churches and all ministries.

With just a little effort and imagination, we can spot denominational officials with or without this gift. Persons with this gift display a special appeal and manner that cause bodies of Christians to want to work together for common goals. Persons lacking this gift often do more damage to cooperative efforts than good. Their good intentions often result in ill-placed energies and plans. They experience more resistance to their efforts than cooperation.

Very few periods in our history have had a more critical need of authentic apostles than today. Our churches in the Western world are declining, and cooperative ministries are suffering shamefully. We seem to have too few heroes of the faith today who can move churches and denominations to work effectively as a united front against evil and disbelief. God still gives spiritual authority and power to certain persons. Let's pray for the grace to recognize and receive today's Pauls and Barnabases (see Acts 14:14).

Battle

The Bible contains many accounts of Spirit-empowered persons who do battle against evil and persons who embody evil. Ephesians 6:11-17 explains how to win against the evil powers. You can find the references for this gift in Gifts' Definitions and Biblical References, page 177.

The definition of battle as a spiritual gift is *the extraordinary ability to use spiritual, physical, and psychological energies and forces to confront and to defeat the evil that hinders the church's call and effectiveness to do God's will.*

The church is at war today, and the evil it faces is not always outside. We recall that Moses came down from Mount Sinai and had to confront the evil of his people (see Exod. 32). The mark of vital faith has always been to challenge immorality, injustice, and heresy within and without. The gift of battle is the might and power to enter into conflicts without losing faith and influence. It is a type of war undergirded by truth but bathed through and through with love.

It is a win-win war and never a win-lose situation. All are victors in the battles in which these gifted persons engage. To be sure, injury and death may occur, but this is not defeat. Under the grace of God, this battle is victory and gain. Often, however, the wrong persons enter conflicts out of too much energy and too little understanding of divine guidance. When they do, no one wins; everyone gets hurt. But when God's gifted soldiers make rank, the results are different. They know when to fight, flight, or strike. They have a special sense to recognize the real enemy. They know when to retreat and to recoup.

Like many pastors, I've had my conflicts. For many years, though, I assumed the responsibility of managing the forces and running the war. I thought that was a part of the pastoral package. I've learned the hard way that I don't have the gift of battle. I don't know how to fight. I can show anyone how to lose, especially without grace! Many persons used the language of the battle gift, saying to me, "Preacher, this is not your battle. Let us fight it for you. We want you to stand back and let us do it." I replied, "Oh, no! I am the general. I don't expect you to lead the troops. That's my job. I'll fight my own wars. I want to be a responsible pastor." The results were devastating, for them and me. I've finally resigned as the general.

God gives certain persons the powerful ability to fight. They do it with efficiency and love. They know that it is better and possible to lose a battle but eventually win a war. They know how to lose in order to win. The outcome is victory for all. They are unlike Elijah, who fled into the wilderness to keep from doing battle with the priests of Baal. They do not behave as Jonah, who ran away from confronting the sinners of

Nineveh. They know that to persevere they need the supportive fellowship of other members. Like Moses, they know they need Aaron. Like Elisha, they see a host of angelic beings guarding God's property (see 2 Kings 6:15-17).

We are at war, but all are not equipped to fight. Let's find the persons with this gift and follow their lead. They know how to destroy their enemies by making them allies.

Craftsmanship

Another often neglected gift, craftsmanship, served the church well for centuries. It is *the extraordinary ability to use physical materials and artistic skills to create, mold, carve, sculpt, draw, design, paint, repair, or photograph items necessary for spiritual nurture, faith development, and caring ministries.*

When we visit the great cathedrals of Europe and Asia, we are awed by earlier Christians' apparent imagination and abilities to produce religious symbolism. The artistic paintings, sculptures, icons, and buildings taught the faith and developed disciples. Modern architecture is sadly lacking in this kind of symbolism. We understand that in most cases the cost is prohibitive today. Yet, we need physical reminders of our faith. The craftsmanship gift can serve us well in other areas.

Craftsmanship covers artworks as well as buildings and equipment for ministry purposes. Today's craftsperson uses special skills to get the most usable and safe buildings for the least cost. Then we can spend our money for aiding persons in need instead of building shrines as idols. Artwork can still aid us in religious education. A prominent manifestation of a rediscovery of this spiritual gift is banner making. It is a lovely, inspiring, and informing experience to see the many banners displayed in some churches.

Something happened in one of my former parishes that brought this gift of craftsmanship to mind. I served a university church, made up of hundreds of professors and students, and I assumed that professors ought to teach in the church school department. After a professor of dentistry and his wife joined the church, I immediately made my request. He said, "No, I won't teach. I have no interest in teaching. If that's all you have for me to do, I'm sorry. Now, if you need any repair work to be done, like replacing windowpanes or door locks, I could get excited about that."

At the time, we were having problems with vandalism and theft. The locks on our doors and windows were out of date, and no replacement parts were available. New hardware was costing us a fortune. When I described the situation to the dentist, he lighted up like a Christmas tree. He assured me that he could make the needed parts in the school's laboratory. Nearly every Saturday afterward he and his wife repaired windows and door locks. I often visited them at work in the church building and found them full of joy and satisfaction over their ministry. Watching a dentist use his dental tools to repair an old door lock was a curious sight.

Bulletin boards present other opportunities for persons with this gift of craftsmanship. The secular world and commercial firms know the value of advertising. Our faith needs the same publicity to draw attention to Christ and his good news. I contend that if we challenge our artists and skilled workers to herald the good news of Christ inside and outside our buildings, we would see amazing results.

Discerning of the Spirits

Discerning of the spirits (Greek, *diakrisis*) is the power to estimate, judge, separate, withdraw from, hesitate, discriminate, oppose, dispute, or be free from doubt. When we mix these ingredients thoroughly and submit them to the energizing power and influence of the Holy Spirit, we experience another form of God's grace. The gift is *the extraordinary ability to know good and evil, right and wrong, and what is either human nature or divine grace; this knowledge is not merely for condemnation but also for the protection and health of the body of Christ.*

I made an interesting discovery in conducting workshops on spiritual gifts: a high percentage of people have this gift. That always surprises me and them. I have often thought that if God had a favorite gift for these days of church decline and crumbling spiritual foundations, it would be evangelism. But for every evangelist, I discover ten spiritual discerners.

I attended a national interdenominational gathering of pastors in San Antonio, Texas. The main speakers came from leadership positions in several denominations. Nearly all warned of the developing faith and social conditions that resemble those of the first century, especially the rising incidence of attacks on church leaders. They described the breakdown of faith in God and one another, persecution of pastors, and schisms within churches, all with unprecedented proportions in modern history. Yet, we are in the midst of a rapid revival and growth of spiritual movements. We can identify over five thousand new movements and religious cults in America. Many persons ask, "How can we sort out what is true and false?"

God may have given many persons the gift of discernment to help us through this confusing maze of doctrines, teachings, theologies, philosophies, and grandiose self-aggrandizement and self-help schemes. Political, economic, philosophical, and theological systems are crumbling all over the world—some for the good and some for the bad. We would do well to translate the Book of Ephesians into a living letter to our situation. We are fighting a war that is not

> against flesh and blood, but against the principalities, against the powers, against the world rulers of this present darkness, against the spiritual hosts of wickedness in the heavenly places.
>
> —Ephesians 6:12

Perhaps the existence of the staggering number of persons who score high on this gift is a sign. Maybe it is time for us to elevate the importance of this gift, find the gifted, and put them to work. What can they do for us? Let's take a look.

Three spiritual forces affect our thinking and behaving. One is of God, another is of the devil, and the third is of human nature. Paul writes of these elements in 1 Corinthians 2: the "wisdom of this age," the "rulers of this age," and the "wisdom of God" (vv. 6-8). He also distinguishes between the "spirit of the world" and the "Spirit which is from God" (2:12). Our problem today is to comprehend this truth.

Every religious organization, denomination, or church emphasizes God's plan and will for life. Most view prophecy as the means of getting this insight. But who is to say who is right and wrong? Anyone can claim to be a speaker for God. Many do. How can we know if they are true or false prophets? In my studies and experience with persons gifted with discernment, I've learned to recognize some characteristics of authentic discerners.

They are not quick to judge behavior or programs that purport to be God's will. Although they may feel things deeply, they have a compassionate power to refrain from judging too hastily. They tend not to seek biblical quotations to confirm their deep feelings but sense the active presence of God as the main source of guidance. Prayerful reflection and spiritual intuiting are internal activities of these persons.

Then, after a period of reflection, they clearly see both sides of issues, which equips them to take a firm stand. This seeing comes from deep feelings of good or bad, right or wrong. Because they cannot always or adequately explain why they are "for" or "against" someone or something, they are often accused of being emotional or illogical. They just know!

Discerners are not always against everything. We often get this impression—but only from inauthentic discernment. True discernment gives feelings of elation and joy when someone or something is right or righteous. These feelings are just as strong and frequent as those of sadness and discomfort when things are not right.

I caution against persons who claim they have discernment when most of their judgments are negative. They are often shocked when I ask for illustrations of good and holy things they have discerned recently. Discernment covers the good of God's spirit as well as the bad of the spirits of the world and human nature.

Another characteristic of persons with discernment is introversion. They often sit in meetings and scan their feelings instead of trying to understand the proceedings. They know that they are elated, glad, sad, or discomforted about persons or things, but they don't always know where these feelings come from. Discerners may be so preoccupied with what is happening internally, they miss details. They are aware of this tendency and choose not to enter into a discussion about details. They do not want to be put on the spot. But when they vote, they know in the heart what is right or wrong. They often go away feeling elated or sad over some action but won't know why. Many feel guilty over their negative feelings.

These persons are of inestimable value because they can save us from following the wrong spirit. I propose this plan. Make sure that at least two persons with this gift are on every committee or board that makes critical decisions. If a sharp division appears in the group over a proposal, ask the discerners *how they feel*. The important thing is not what they know but what they feel—good or bad, high or low—about the group's readiness to vote. If both of them say "bad," ask the group to delay the vote and take this issue before God in prayer. Few things are so urgent that a few days of prayer cannot be given. If one of them says "bad" and the other says "good," I suggest an immediate period of prayer to help the members get in touch with the reality of God's spirit who cares about what is happening.

After prayer, take a poll of the members to see if they are ready to vote. A poll is not an official vote but a nonthreatening way of learning where group members are. A sharp division in the body of Christ on any issue can cause irreparable harm. A poll indicates the level of divisiveness or agreement. The gift of discernment can help us as catalysts to engage this procedure for eventual unity.

I have discovered some statistical characteristics of this gift. Among the hundreds of clergy spouses who filled out the Grace-Gifts Discovery Inventory, approximately 90 percent scored highest on this gift. My wife is one of them. Could it be that God, in calling certain persons to the ordained ministry, knew they needed special protection? Long before I seriously listened to my wife as one who has the gift, she warned me about things and persons. How I wish now that I had listened to her then! Also, more females than males have discernment, and more laity than clergy have this gift.

Surely God's will involves every person and thing that touches the body of Christ. Nothing is beyond the reach of divine love. Therefore, it is conceivable that the enemy will invade the little and imperceptible things while the group's energy and attention focus on big and important matters. We know, though, that enough of these small things can contaminate the whole. The gift of discernment helps to flush out these overlooked and unattended hindrances to perfecting God's will for the church.

But look out for abuses of this gift! They abound. Satan can—and does—counterfeit any good thing. Persons with this gift ought to get together and pray together for one another and for the proper use of their gift. This way they can offer a ministry to the body of Christ that no other gift offers. We should never take for granted that because a good person is working, everything he or she does is right or righteous. The measure of rightness or righteousness is always the good done for the whole church, not for some individuals. Evil always elevates the importance of one or more parts over others. Evil triumphs only when good people are not aware of the presence of evil. Evil is defeated when righteousness prevails. The gift of discernment can aid us in this endeavor.

Evangelism

"Evangelism" comes from the Greek *euangelizamai*, meaning "to declare," "to announce," "to proclaim," or "to present good news to win new persons to Christ." Although used less than we would guess in the New Testament, it is one of the richest Greek words to express jubilation over some great gain or liberation from some great hindrance. While the noun form (*euangelistes*) is used only three times in reference to persons (see Acts 21:8; Eph. 4:11; 2 Tim. 4:5), it describes the whole New Testament. It is the good news of Jesus Christ who died and was resurrected to procure for us salvation (wholeness) in a living relationship with God now and for eternity.

The definition of evangelism for our purposes here is *the extraordinary ability to give such a witness to the love of God as expressed in Jesus Christ that it moves others to accept that love and to become disciples of Christ.* Through the efforts of the evangelist, new birth into the kingdom of God is made possible.

In examining the roles of various gifts, we realize that some prepare the soil (to use the agricultural metaphor), others do the planting, still others water and nourish, and the harvesting is the pleasure of others (see 1 Cor. 3:5-6). The evangelist effectively harvests souls for Christ through faithful witnessing.

Understanding the connection between evangelist, teacher, apostle, and pastor is necessary. If we follow Paul's analogy of the human anatomy to understand the church as the body of Christ, we have to acknowledge that no single part or member can do all the work of the body. In the process of giving birth, one organ—the uterus—does that, but the whole body gives life.

The evangelist has the power to give birth to new disciples, but the whole church gives life. I have heard denominational officials try to motivate ordained ministers to new heights of ministry by telling them that all pastors are evangelists, all pastors are apostles, all pastors are teachers, and so on.

Yet, all parts of the human body are required to reproduce its kind. The same is true of the church as the body of Christ. One gift cannot approximate the work and power of another. Although the New Testament is the good news (*euangelion*) of God through Christ, a specific part of it is designated the Gospels. The same is true of the church. The whole church is *the* evangelist—the good news agency—but a certain part of that body does the major part of the birthing. The pastor oversees the spiritual needs before, during, and after. The teacher instructs the body on how all parts connect and work for a common goal. The apostle goes beyond the immediate environment to capture the imagination and involvement of others. The administrator puts together personnel and materials to provide for nourishment and growth. The exhorter comforts and encourages all involved, including the new convert. And on it goes. This simple scan shows that life depends on more than just birth, but the evangelist does the birthing.

The evangelist perceives when the time of harvest is ready. I am acquainted with an evangelist who knows by name over three thousand persons he helped to be born again. He said that he has a special sense of when the time is right, when the birth is ready to take place. He is careful not to force the process too soon. Sometimes, he says, it takes a long spiritual gestation period. With others, the period is not that long. He has learned, though, to treat each prospect according to the person's unique situation and process. Standardized formulas applied to all births do not produce the best births.

The authentic evangelist will not allow church growth statistics or leadership to set the date and number of new births. He or she will pay attention to the divine process and never try birthing until it is time. That is, the evangelist knows by divine intuition and initiation when a person is ready. There is no wholesale and mass birthing in the kingdom of God, but there is new birth (see John 3:3).

Sometimes, however, because of ill spiritual health in the body of believers, birth is hindered, and the evangelist must act under unfavorable circumstances. The pastor, as shepherd, often knows of the unhealthy condition and is hesitant to encourage the body to reproduce its kind. He or she will attempt other ministries to raise the health of the body, but some traditionalists insist on a revival to win new souls. The church calls an evangelist. Prospects for new birth are always available, and the visiting evangelist becomes the midwife to facilitate the birthing. In many cases, the body, still in its ill health, neglects the postnatal nourishment, and the mortality rate of spiritual infants increases. Conversion becomes another dead statistic.

Often, by default and out of thwarted efforts, persons gifted as evangelists strike out beyond the body of Christ to independent means and methods of fulfilling their calling. Unfortunately, their meetings mass-produce spiritual orphans. It is well documented that a very small percentage of their converts are nurtured by the churches. To be sure, some evangelists have an inordinate need for self-gain and popularity. They are counterfeits, and many souls are ruined by their efforts.

Authentic evangelists, as chosen instruments of God, are not always preachers. Most are laypersons. They are interested in others' spiritual welfare and know the importance of their church in the nurture of the converts. They know that the dedication at the altar is only the beginning and not a statistical end. Their main concern is not what the newly born Christians can do for the church but what the church, as Christ's body, can do for them.

The authentic evangelist uses the Bible as a means of revealing to people the love God offers through Christ for healing and wholeness. The true evangelist enjoys a simple definition of religion and is not too fond of the complex dimensions of theology.

Persons with this gift faithfully work in the local church and have a high record of attendance. They enjoy familiar music and hymns with sounds and messages that move others toward a warm, vivid experience with Christ. During the sermons they pray for hearts to be touched and lives to be changed by the service. They want the preacher to give an invitation after each sermon. The pastor with this gift will always give a call for commitment after the sermon. Laypersons with this gift will often leave a church that doesn't practice the call to commitment. They want to see people changed by the services.

Problems accompany this gift. Sometimes these persons cannot understand why other Christians do not have their enthusiasm for leading people to Christ. Caught off guard, they may criticize others for not evangelizing. Also, these gifted persons may appear to be more concerned about the sins of the prospect than the person as an individual. Some converts express disappointment over not receiving further attention and care from the evangelist who won them to Christ.

Perhaps a single major problem with the gift of evangelism is that many of the gifted show too little concern for other needs, such as social, economic, medical, international, political, educational, and environmental. Somehow, evangelists tend to think that relating persons to Christ as Savior is the solution for the world's ills. Consequently, within the body of Christ, they show little concern for the other dimensions of body life. These are problems only when the evangelists forget or overlook the varieties of other gifts designed and distributed by the same Lord.

The most impressive result of this gift is body growth. The church either grows or dies. With active persons obediently practicing this gift, the church grows. This statement also applies to the pastor whose dominant gift is evangelism. The charismatic power that accompanies this gift attracts more persons into the kingdom of God. In pastoral visitation, one truly enjoys visiting prospects for Christ and the body of Christ, the church. This type of ministry initiates and maintains body growth, not by design as much as by the nature of the gift. Wise leaders of any local church would do well to identify these gifted persons and provide ample opportunities for them to fulfill their calling in the community.

7

All That You Ever Wanted to Know About Gifts

Exhortation

"Exhortation," from the Greek *parakaleo* or *paraklesis*, is a cousin of a New Testament word for "Holy Spirit," *paraclete*, translated "comforter" or "strong companion." The word has two parts: one is "a call," and the other is "companionship." Together, they form a ministry of "being with and for another." The meaning of this gift includes standing by, sitting with, guiding, encouraging, strengthening, inspiring, motivating, consoling, begging, urging, and comforting.

The definition for this gift is *the extraordinary ability to inspire, encourage, and strengthen others in and through their efforts to live out God's will and calling as Christians in pain and pleasure, want and plenty.* (See Gifts' Definitions and Biblical References, page 177, for the biblical references.)

Christian living is no easy undertaking. God neither made it so nor promised that it would be. The models of our Lord and all who initially followed him should remind us that the Way is no bed of roses. Yet, it's possible with promises of joy, fulfillment, and completion (see John 15:11; 16:24; Rom. 8:37-39).

God equips the church with members who are powerful in their ministry of encouragement. A person's well-placed word with the right tone of voice, facial expression, and body movement can lift another from depression to new vigor and direction.

Everyone knows the power of a loving word, a compassionate gesture, or even the silent presence of another who effectively communicates love. I know medical doctors and surgeons who often see greater results from the use of words of hope and encouragement than from medicine or surgery. How powerful is the influence of someone with the gift of exhortation!

Although it is right to expect all members of the body of Christ to encourage one another, some have the special power to build up confidence and competence within the church by their presence and words. A study of these persons reveals certain behavioral characteristics.

They are often quick to speak a word of caution or instruction as well as comfort but with an unmistakable spirit of caring. They are more concerned about the person or group to whom they minister than any project or event involved. They are person-centered and goal-oriented. That is, their first love is to equip persons with positive attitudes and feelings about themselves and their relationship with God. Next, they know the value of persevering to the end, whatever it may be.

The exhorters know from intuition and deep feelings how to be "with" and "for" others, and the others sense this. Unlike the gift of teaching, the verbal content of their encouragement is more emotional than directive. In a real sense, they become the strong force that overcomes weakness of persons to whom they minister. This ministry is similar to our Lord's promise of the *paraclete*, the Holy Spirit, as "one who is called to be along side of you" (John 14:16, AP).

The counselor or comforter does not intend or desire to rescue a hurting person from a pain-producing situation but yearns to be the weak's strength or the lonely's companion. The encourager sees value in the process of working through the problem to its completion. Persons with this gift often spend much time with persons in need of motivation rather than those who need instruction. In fact, others sense this tendency in them and seek them out. Many wind up in counseling professions and ministries.

Barnabas is our best illustration of someone with this gift in the New Testament. In Acts 4:36-37 Luke is eager to show how Barnabas came about his name as "Son of encouragement." His example, not verbal teaching, inspired others to do the hard work of discipleship, which included sacrificial giving. In this case, Barnabas did not preach or teach how Christians ought to give of their means. He sold a piece of property and laid the money at the apostles' feet.

At another time Barnabas went after Paul, who had disappeared, because he knew others needed Paul's gifts in Antioch. Instead of assuming a role of leadership for himself in Antioch, he searched for Paul and brought him back to give the instructions needed. The gift of exhortation often serves as a coach. The coach does not play the game but knows how to get others to do it.

Another example of Barnabas's encouragement is his defense of Mark's ministry, even against Paul's refusal (see Acts 15:36-41). Paul had an unpleasant experience with Mark's earlier abandonment and refused to have anything else to do with him. Barnabas insisted on taking Mark with him on his mission to strengthen the churches. We need not elaborate on who was right in this matter. This characteristic is typical of exhortation: getting involved with the down-and-outers, weak sisters and brothers.

Churches urgently need to discover persons with this gift of encouragement. I am no prophet, but the logic of my gift of teaching, the insights from my gift of knowledge, and the heart of my gift of exhortation cry out on behalf of the church. Coming soon is a period of unprecedented confusion and pain for the church in America. It has already begun with the twenty-five years of declining membership, the fall of superevangelists, and the increasing harsh attacks on pastors. One tactic of the evil one is to discredit or wound the shepherd (pastor); then the flock becomes confused and scattered. The church requires all gifts, but some periods call for certain ones more than others. We have had centuries of good instruction and skillful organization. Today's great need is for encouragers, those who will stick with us and share their strength. We can use not more light bearers but more persons who can keep our light from going out.

Exorcism

We should not be surprised to find this gift included, especially since so many movies have been made about demon possession and Satan worship, and so many books on the same subjects have been published.

Many psychiatrists and psychologists are calling us to reexamine the viability of intentional exorcism. They have discovered illnesses of mind and powers that cripple and destroy for which there is no physical explanation or cure apart from spiritual realities. The New Testament contains many illustrations and descriptions of exorcism. Yet, a large segment of Christianity remains silent and indifferent toward this subject.

One reason for this indifference is our attachment to a scientific worldview, which does not permit us to attribute any cause for an effect to anything beyond what can be measured and analyzed by scientific methodology. Our restriction of much of our present-day practice of the Christian faith to whatever is scientifically acceptable is a carryover from Aristotle, who taught that reality rests only in the senses and that nothing deserves our attention unless it relates to what can be seen, tasted, touched, smelled, and heard. But we all know that there is more to life.

An article in a scientific journal said in essence: No intelligent person can read the evidence for the existence of ESP and doubt that it exists; but, since we know it is impossible, we must conclude that all this evidence is due to error and fraud. Christians often apply this illogic to their practice of faith. I know many persons who would never read a book on spiritual gifts, to say nothing of one that considers the possibility of evil spirits and demons. However, these same people agree that science fails to offer any help in these matters, which they cannot easily dismiss.

Jesus apparently believed in forces that did not come from the physical world. He and others often confronted these powerful spiritual realities. According to the Gospels, Jesus conversed with angels and demons. Who are we to say that Jesus was wrong, insane, or psychotic? Paul's writings are full of descriptions and explanations of ill conditions caused by alien spirits and forces. Are we to say that he was disoriented?

If either Jesus or Paul is merely using cultural beliefs and language of the day to communicate something else, how are we to value anything else he says to us? Jesus, Paul, and many others knew of spiritual realities that could improve or destroy human life. The only way to some healings was a spiritual force, and the only way for some liberations was a spiritual exorcism.

"Exorcism" comes from the Greek word *exorkistes* and its various forms found throughout the New Testament. It basically means "to drive out," "to expel," "to cast out," "to force out," "to release," "to call forth," "to diffuse," "to extricate," "to free." The definition of the gift is *the ability to use various means of faith, prayers, spirit-music, and other gifts to liberate persons from evil-centered hindering forces so that they may be in effective ministry to and for the body of Christ.*

This definition does not necessarily mean that one person has all these gifts but is able to organize his or her gifts along with others' gifts for the exorcising operation. If, however, one person apparently has these gifts for the operation of exorcism, he or she finds that the special abilities do not appear when attempting to operate in other ministry situations.

According to biblical records, some demonic or evil forces require forms of treatment that differ from the spiritual gift of healing. We need to be careful here not to think that every illness of mind or body comes from demonic forces. Being possessed by an evil spirit is not a normal illness, nor is it a purely psychological phenomenon. It is a powerful entrenchment of an alien force. All known medical treatments cannot liberate persons from it. Many medications may sedate victims for a period but do not cure them. Many psychiatrists report cases others labeled demon possession but turned out to be treatable illness of mind and body. Other Christian psychiatrists, psychologists, and missionaries find that the healing or deliverance from evil forces comes only through means that powerfully convey *agape* love and grace.

The New Testament depicts this ministry of deliverance, and further accounts are found beyond the New Testament, throughout the Middle Ages, and into the present age. These accounts are not restricted to the illiterate and the superstitious. We would not consider medical doctors, psychologists, and highly trained missionaries among the superstitious. Yet, many of them report conditions that can be explained only as demon possession.

Abuses of this gift cause many persons to abandon its practice. The abuses appear in magical formulas, incantations, brews, and esoteric rituals. Power-hungry people develop incomprehensible rituals and leave their hapless subjects (victims) either in awe or in awful turmoil. I don't mean to suggest that abuses always fail and quacks never succeed. Jesus warns in Matthew 7:22-23 that many will claim entry into the kingdom because of their good works, one of which is exorcism. They even cast out demons in the name of Jesus, which indicates that they were successful. The warning is against the abusers, not the persons actually delivered.

To expel demons, our Lord used the power and authority of "a word" (Matt. 8:16). His disciples patterned their ministry after his example but did it in the name of Jesus (see Mark 16:17; Luke 10:17). Their method of delivering people from evil forces then is a far cry from the ways many claim to do it today.

We should be concerned about these practices, but we should also be concerned about the reluctance of reasonable and informed Christians to comment on the possibility of actual demon possession today. When I spoke with some colleagues about the possibility, none made an out-and-out denial that there is such a thing. But the response was timid and confused. A deeper discussion with a few of them revealed their own dark night of the soul they believed to be of a power human efforts cannot cure. A pill cannot touch some illnesses of mind and body.

C. S. Lewis has helped us to overcome the perception of the devil with horns and a forked tail by describing him, as the Bible does, as an angel of light. Nevertheless, more than fiction and masterful writings are required to deliver us from the satanic forces binding us. Our Lord is in that business and apportions to certain persons the gift of exorcism. With their aid, we can be delivered from the clutches of evil.

How do people know if they have the gift? This gift carries a yearning to free others from an obvious enslavement to evil. These persons usually have the companion gift of discernment, the ability to distinguish between what is of God, of human nature, and of evil. In all probability, they have the gifts of mercy and exhortation. Exorcism, therefore, may be more a combination of these gifts than a single gift. It brings to the recipients a power to judge between what is commonly and forgivably sinful and what is demonically enslaving.

Though others make light of certain sins or acts of disobedience, the gifted person sees the long-term effects of destruction. This person feels a pull toward one who is enslaved by an evil power and yearns to assist with deliverance. Often, when speaking to the possessed person, the gifted will say something like this, "Let me help you to be delivered from this condition. Share it with me and let's get rid of it."

The gift causes the gifted to absorb or to receive the evil condition of the possessed. The demonic power passes from the possessed to the gifted and diminishes immediately under the powerful presence of grace and love. Sometimes, the one that was possessed is so relieved that he or she goes limp or is temporarily rendered unconscious (some call this condition being slain in the Spirit). Sometimes, the gifted is so shocked by the absorption of the evil power that he or she goes limp or becomes unconscious. The resulting peace for both is extraordinary and lasting.

Faith

Doesn't everyone have faith? Yes, but the gift of faith is different. A general faith is basic to our relationship with God and Christian discipleship. A gift of faith *is an extraordinary ability to extend general or saving faith to serve corporate and individual needs specifically related to church life as the body of Christ.* The main difference is not in kind but in degree.

The Greek word *pistis*, in reference to Christ, denotes a strong conviction (mental assent) about and dedication (discipleship) to Jesus Christ as God's gift of redemption. It is through this attachment to Christ that God's grace brings forgiveness for sins and eternal life. No person can be in a right relationship with God without this basic faith.

The Holy Spirit energizes and empowers this basic faith in certain members of the church to be channels for powerful operations (miracles) needed for building up the body. Acts 11:22-24 describes Barnabas as "full of the Holy Spirit and of faith." Why "faith" here? Can a person have the Holy Spirit without faith? No, but the author of the Book of Acts speaks of Barnabas's extraordinary dimension of faith, a special spiritual gift of faith. A "large company" came to believe in Christ as a result of Barnabas's extended use of faith.

We recognize this gift in persons who are well-seasoned Christians and who demonstrate their faith in powerful works. They are persons with childlike faith; that is, they believe something without questioning. They have a special sense or feeling about a thing that it is the will of God.

They speak of God's will about certain issues, events, projects, or needs instead of calling for prayer or biblical confirmations. They seem to know what God wants to happen without searching or petitioning God in prayer. They rarely feel a need to find biblical proof or confirmation to undergird their faith force. Others may misunderstand, thinking that they discount the Bible and prayer. To the contrary, they often pray diligently about certain matters. Once they have discovered God's will, though, more praying is redundant. "It is finished!"

Another peculiarity of this gift is that the recipients would rather believe God is going to do something than jump in and do it themselves. A professor of physics at a university where I was the pastor of a university church obviously had an intimate relationship with God. On several occasions he came to tell me that some project was OK to pursue. I would ask, "How do you know that we can swing it? Are you going to do it?" He would answer, "It's OK. Let's go on with it." I would press harder until he told me that his faith said that God was going to make it happen. The surprise was that it did happen! I learned from him that he had prayed about the matter until he found answers.

These persons with the spiritual gift of faith do not have to go through ritualistic exercises to appropriate the results of their faith. They do not offer prayers in a certain act (e.g., at an altar in a sanctuary) or formula (e.g., with meditative exercises). They simply focus their basic faith (visualization) on the project or need, and suddenly they "know" whether God's will favors it. Their faith is no excuse for laziness or sloth. They never walk away from a needed ministry with the attitude that says, "God will do it. Let it alone. Go on about your business." No, they begin to live and behave as though the object of their faith has already happened. Their visualization leads to actualization in their behavior. The hallmark of their belief system is trust (see Mark 11:24).

An abuse of this gift is projecting it onto others. Some abusers tend to say to others who do not have the gift, "Where is your faith?" or "Can't you trust God?" One of the saintliest persons I know told me of a scar she carried twenty years. She gave birth to a stillborn child, and a Christian friend and neighbor said to her, "If you had faith, this would not have happened." Persons with this gift of extraordinary faith should be careful about what they say to others. The gift of faith is never to judge another's faith. It is to allow one's faith to be a channel of God's grace to bring God's will and fulfillment to another's life. A nonabusive way of speaking to the bereaved parent would have been, "God is with you and is trusting you with this great loss. God's grace is powerful to work a miracle in your life."

Giving

This gift, sometimes translated "generosity" or "liberality," comes from the Greek word *metadidomi*, meaning "to turn over," "to give over," "to share," "to transfer," "to deliver from one's substance to the needs of another." The scriptural references for this gift are noted in Gifts' Definitions and Biblical References, page 177.

Giving is a basic standard of service for every Christian, but there is evidence that God gives to certain ones an extraordinary sense of others' needs and the power to do something about it. The power, in many cases, demonstrates itself in the ability to acquire more and more resources out of which more and more substances can be given.

Giving is *the ability to manage one's resources of income, time, energy, and skills to exceed what is considered to be a reasonable standard for giving to the church, an amount that brings joy and power to do more for further service.*

The behavioral traits of this charismatic generosity include the intense desire and motivation to give and special abilities and opportunities to give abundantly. While giving manifests itself beyond money, if it is money, one's ability and opportunity to make money accompany the gift.

Giving also brings ecstasy, whether it covers time, skills, or money. Most English translations use "cheerfulness," which comes from the Greek *hilarotes* that describes something with an extra amount of joy or freedom. "Hilarious" comes from that, meaning "out of mind and all over oneself." We often use this word to describe a full laughing response to something funny. In short, it is sharing with extraordinary self-abandonment or denial, giving that feels good.

Persons with this gift do not give for recognition or publicized trophies; they do it quietly and without fanfare. When recognition is offered to givers, they may consent only if it motivates others to do their share—whether or not the others have the gift. The gift of liberality usually alerts persons to valid and worthy needs that may, in the ordinary course of events, be overlooked by others. They experience joy when they learn that their services are answers to specific prayers and needs. They are never stingy in sharing and tie no strings to their offerings unless they perceive a potential abuse.

Persons with this *charisma* maintain a positive attitude toward the church's continuous need for financial assistance and are systematic in their support. They never sigh, "There they go again, and here I come to the rescue again." They rarely have second thoughts about the worthiness of the recipients of their givings, as long as they aid the church's ministry.

I know of a golfer who won twenty thousand dollars. As he left the clubhouse for the parking lot, he saw a young woman crying and wanted to know why. She told him that her child was sick and needed an expensive operation and that she had no insurance. The champion golfer was so moved by her apparent sincerity and plight that he endorsed the check and gave it to her. Someone else saw what happened and eventually told him that he had been conned. The woman had no child and had gotten money from others with a similar ploy. He replied, "You mean, you really mean that there is no child who is that ill and in need of expensive surgery?" "Yes," answered his informant. The golfer exclaimed, "This is the best news yet! I am thankful to God that there is no sick child." The gift of liberality is extraordinary in many ways. One dimension is that "it is more blessed to give than to receive" (Acts 20:35).

In most cases, these gifted people are not wealthy in time, skills, or money, but they always give beyond reasonable limits. When their offerings are abused or misused, their fulfillment is no less to them. Their joy is in the process of turning loose and giving forth. In Romans 12:8 the Greek word that accompanies the gift of giving is *haploteti*, which is translated "self-abandonment," "singleness of eye," "simple kindness out of the sheer joy of giving." It often includes sacrifice but not without an amount of joy that can sustain and motivate further liberality. A person doesn't have to be wealthy to give. The widow's mite is an apt illustration (see Luke 21:2).

After one of my workshops on the gifts, during which an aged widow discovered she had the gift of giving, she gave her pastor a large check for a piece of property the church had needed for a long time. The officials of the church became concerned. They returned the check and said, "We don't want to take your money. You can't do this." She replied with vigor,

"Do you mean to say that you'll stand in my way of receiving such a joy in giving? Don't you dare keep me from the joy God wants me to have!"

If persons with this spiritual gift are in a right relationship with Christ, they don't brag about what they give or criticize others for what they don't give. They are willing to maintain a lower standard of living or to do without something to contribute more to the church's ministries. They never give any thought to buying attention or recognition from God and others by generous giving of time, skills, and money. They never attempt to dictate spending policies of the church. Once they have given, they feel it is up to God and other servants to administer their gifts.

The biblical standard for giving is the tithe, which is ten percent. As it is with all the spiritual gifts (*charismata*), the gift of giving is energized and made extraordinary by the Holy Spirit only as it is done. We cannot know if we have the spiritual gift of liberality until we have exceeded a standard expectation. If our spiritual gift is giving, God will provide the resources to do the impossible.

8

Grace upon Grace

John 1:16 asserts, "And from his fulness have we all received, grace upon grace." There is no end to it. God keeps pouring out divine love to us. So we continue to examine manifestations of it through the grace-gifts (*charismata*), extraordinary abilities to build up the body of Christ.

Healings

The New Testament words for "healings" are *iamaton* and *therapeia*, meaning "cures" or "serving to make whole." The specific reference to a spiritual gift for healing is 1 Corinthians 12:9, which is *iamaton*, a plural form. The verb form means "to cure or be cured" or "to make or be made whole," and it goes beyond physical illnesses to include mind, emotions, society, morals, theology, and philosophy. The specific scriptural references appear in Gifts' Definitions and Biblical References, page 177.

The definition of this spiritual gift is *the extraordinary ability God gives to certain members of the body of Christ to cure or to be cured of ill conditions that hinder effective ministries for Christ, the church, or individuals*. This definition narrows the scope of divine healing to a perspective not always articulated by the church. My contention is that God gives a healing ministry to the church, apart from secular and medical practices, to free the church of hindrances to fulfill its commission (see Matt. 28:19-20). This intent is different from that of secular therapy, which is also a gift of God (not *charisma*).

I know of few things that get more abuse than prayers for and expectations of healings. In over three hundred churches I have visited, only a few omitted any reference to prayers for the physically ill. Some ninety-nine percent of all requests for prayers I heard were for some physical illness.

Biblical terms for healing cover much more than the body. In our North American culture where we pray for body health more than any other subject, Christians do not live longer than non-Christians, despite the multitude of testimonies of divine healings to the contrary. A serious question concerns whether most Christians even have a quality of life that others do not have. I believe the church's ability to fulfill its commission to make disciples (see Matt. 28:19-20) hinges upon healing and wholeness; the church needs a better understanding of the charismatic offering of healings.

As it is with the other spiritual gifts, healings build up the church for effective ministries. They are not merely to deliver an individual from misery, pain, discomfort, or suffering. Spiritual gifts often associated with healings may also bring wholeness instead. There is a difference, which we will discuss later (see "suffering," chapter 12). I believe if we could ever settle this misunderstanding, miraculous healings would be the order of the day.

The person with the spiritual gift of healing discerns any unhealthy condition that hinders the progress and wholeness of the church's ministry. Though the condition may be an illness of an individual, the healer knows that the health of that person is necessary for the wholeness of the body of Christ. Also, the authentic healer's concern, going beyond the physical condition of the sick, may be a means to win the person to Christ, not merely to rid him or her of pain.

Another trait of the authentic healer is sensitivity to the will of God. He or she will never claim that God's will is that all should be healed, as most wholesale radio and television evangelist-healers claim. That claim is not biblical.

The Bible records many accounts of suffering designed for God to bring about a greater good. There are too many splendid Christians today who know their ill conditions are God's will to deny this greater good. Healing here may be of the mind, that is, aiding someone to accept an illness as God's gift. I call this wholeness rather than healing. To be whole is to accept God's will whatever it brings, even ill health and pain.

This acceptance is not a passive posture toward an ill condition but a dramatic gift that brings an extraordinary amount of joy and meaning to any situation.

Authentic healers stand a chance of being misunderstood as they explain that some conditions of illness bring about this greater good for the kingdom. Perhaps for this reason many authentic healers have the accompanying gifts of exhortation, discerning of spirits, faith, and wisdom.

These persons do not always know the effects of the use of their gift. When they do learn of them, they have no need to publicize their importance. They will not publicly reveal the contents of letters extolling their ministry. They are not interested in trying to prove their case. They are willing to let God handle the consequences. Very rarely do the real healers hold healing crusades with fanfare and personalized billing. This approach is totally contrary to their understanding of healing as belonging to the body of Christ, the church.

Often in a quiet and meditative manner, sometimes with laying on of hands and sometimes not, the healer prays. Many times the true healer hurts deeply when too much emphasis is put on physical illness, knowing full well that many requests are self-centered and hedonistic. Also, healers will wonder why pastors do not lift up the healing aspects of God's grace. They know that healing is as necessary as teaching, evangelizing, and music.

Healers are attracted to the healing stories in the Bible, especially those involving our Lord. They look for meanings of those healings larger than the release of suffering. They are also attracted to services that offer opportunities for healing and wholeness. When they witness a healing conducted by someone else or hear of others, they react not with suspicion and doubt but with joyful thanksgiving to God. They are, however, often critical of persons who claim to have been healed but are not intimately and serviceably related to the church's active ministries. Their foundation in the Bible provides an understanding of healing as being given by God for a purpose related to the kingdom.

Gifts of healing may not always be something done to or for others; they may also be something received. The plural form of "gifts" here, found in 1 Corinthians 12:9, may explain why some persons are healed many times, perhaps for the same or similar condition. And as with persons who are gifted to heal others, the recipients of healing as a gift have certain behavioral characteristics.

They deeply sense their need to be at their best in ministry to the church. Their request for healing comes not from a simple, selfish longing to be well and free of discomfort but from a desire to be functional in their services to the church. They do not always think in terms of healing for relief from suffering; sometimes they consider healing a means of influencing others to turn to Christ. Many of them say that they had rather be sick to win persons to Christ than to be well and barren in disciple making.

I know a person who has been sick and healed more times than it is possible to count. Her illnesses and healings have won hundreds of persons to Christ—doctors, nurses, workers in hospitals, and visitors. She has called me many times and said, "Here I am again, with another cancer and in the hospital. Pray that I will win more to Christ."

We do not know why some persons are healed and others are not. We can only guess. One guess is that some people are not properly related to the body of Christ and therefore cannot receive the benefits of God's grace for which the church is a channel. Another guess is that some people do not want to be healed; they want only attention. We do know, though, that healing is a ministry of the church and has been since its beginning. It is not something private between the sick and God.

We should not be embarrassed over persons we fail to heal any more than those we fail to convert or educate. We should, however, be very concerned if we do not provide opportunities for persons to discover their gifts and use them to vitalize all ministries of the body. Christians who are not healed should not think of themselves as inferior to others or stigmatized by God; they should open themselves to a further and deeper understanding of God's will for their lives.

One of the saintliest persons I have ever known, a person whose faith and practice the whole community depended upon, was diagnosed with cancer. In spite of all the praying for her healing, she died. Before she died, she sent for me, although I wasn't her pastor. I dreaded going to see her because she was getting sicker, and I did not know how to handle this "failure." I learned immediately upon entering her bedroom that illness and death are not archenemies of faith. A glow from the radiance of a smile on her face lighted the whole room. I did not have to minister to her at all; she ministered to me. She said, "Brother Charles, God has trusted me with a cancer." The cancer became her port of entry into the eternal presence of our Lord. Sometimes, therefore, carcinoma is *charisma*. A friend of mine says, "Everybody wants to go to heaven, but nobody wants to die!" Death is our ultimate healing.

Helps

This word comes from *antilempsis* in Greek and is found only once in the New Testament: 1 Corinthians 12:28. Paul lists it as one of the spiritual gifts. It means "to aid and assist another in need." A deeper understanding of it comes from another word, *antilambanesthai*, which describes a reciprocity between one who is helping and one who is helped (see Acts 20:35).

The gift is reciprocal in that the receiver does as much for the giver as the giver does for the receiver. The giver and the receiver are on equal par.

Not a passive acceptance of help, this reception equally rewards the giver with a sense of completion and joy. A partial understanding may be found in the saying, "It is more blessed to give than to receive" (Acts 20:35). What is true in this gift is that "it is as blessed to give as to receive." The definition, therefore, is *the extraordinary ability to aid others in need in such a way that the giver receives as much as the receivers get.*

Some people may confuse this gift with that of service, which will be discussed later. Helps centers on the needs of another person or other persons, but service centers on the worship of God. Although both may be the same act or deed, the motivation is different.

Persons with the spiritual gift of helps feel compelled to give from their skills, talents, and energy to help others who have an apparent need. They delight not so much in what they do for others as in the relationship with the others. They rarely question the legitimacy of the needed aid. They see the persons in need not as objects of charity but as participants in an intimate relationship in the body of Christ.

The helpers feel that they have done something for themselves when they help others. Their aid becomes a sacred form of communication between themselves and the persons helped. Their assistance gives birth to warm feelings toward the ones they help, never a sense of superiority. They often give aid not because they love but because they want to love. Thus, the recipients feel apprehended by a force greater than both parties—the presence of the living Christ: "I was hungry and you gave me food, I was thirsty and you gave me drink" (Matt. 25:35).

That we find this spiritual gift in abundance in all churches should be no surprise since there are so many ways everyone can be helped. Apparently, this gift is greatly needed because of the low self-esteem of many Christians. Persons receiving the ministry of helps sense that they are, indeed, important and special to get such attention.

Hospitality

Hospitality here does not refer to good cooks or workers in the kitchen, as important as they are. Many churches have hospitality committees, and some have a professional hostess who arranges fellowship dinners. The spiritual gift of hospitality does not function in this way. The word *philonexia* in Greek means "love or fondness of strangers" and is made up of two words: *philos*, meaning "friendliness," "accepting," and "openness"; and *zenos*, meaning "stranger," "alien," or "outsider." The definition of the gift is *the extraordinary ability God gives certain persons to extend caring and sharing to persons (strangers) beyond their intimate circle to demonstrate and to establish the unlimited and inclusive companionship of Christ.* Scriptural references may be found in Gifts' Definitions and Biblical References, page 177.

Human beings are territorial creatures; we tend to protect our ground or habitat from unfamiliar and unwanted intruders. We go beyond mere geography to include ideas, rituals, and groupings based on similar and compatible affinities. The most primitive groupings, family and religious cults, were not to be invaded by unwelcomed persons without extreme challenges by their leaders. Boundaries were rigid and sacred. This nature manifests itself in current fraternities, sororities, guilds, clubs, classes, tribes, cults, and religions.

Christianity was to be different. Its motif was the great commission to evangelize "all people," *ta ethne* (see Matt. 28:19-20), to offer special loving attention to aliens and strangers. While other cults and religions did not and could not reach out to outsiders, this characteristic was the genius and heart of the Christian "Way" (John 3:16). Consequently, certain members of the body of Christ received a special grace of God (*charisma*) that empowers them to reach out, attract, and receive strangers openly and winsomely. The key to this empowerment comes from the Greek *diokontes* that appears with "hospitality" in Romans 12:13 but often is translated "practice." "Practice" is too weak to catch the import of this gift, for it literally means "to run after," "to pursue or promote," "to hasten toward," or "to capture."

These charismatically empowered persons attract outsiders by showing a sincere concern for them. They tend to prefer to be with strangers or the uninitiated. They delight in meeting new persons. They are quick to respond to special needs of strangers, such as lodging, food, entertainment, and companionship. They do not hesitate to initiate an offer of help. They rarely fear any threat from approaching strangers.

Once they have established a relationship with strangers or visitors, they tend to move on to others. Sometimes they appear gushy toward visitors or strangers and are interpreted as coming on too strong. Persons with this gift often appear to be bored with or negligent toward established friendships in their attempts to devote time and energy to new persons. When they converse with strangers, they usually center on the stranger's needs and desires rather than on what the program or group has in mind. They are person-centered and not program- or group-centered.

They usually feel more comfortable in short-term relationships than in longer ones. Neatness of place (home or church) or excellence of program (church) is not a prime consideration with them when they invite guests. They consider establishing a new relationship the essential transaction, not the meal or bed in the home, and not the service or program in the church. This love of strangers often endures and delights in personal hardship to serve guests.

Persons with this gift are not always the tidiest people we know. They may be so interested in their guests as persons that they overlook cleaning the walkway or house. They are not entertainers and performers. They are strictly people persons. They do not easily fret over details and preparations. The guests or visitors may find dishes in the sink, beds unmade, and toys scattered throughout the house. Many without this gift would be horrified over such conditions and often make everyone miserable while preparing for their guests.

This ministry has great value in the church. These persons see people as the business of the church, not its programs and organizations. To them, getting new people into the body brings new vitality and spiritual health. To welcome strangers is to welcome Christ (see Matt. 25:35, 38, 40).

The difference between this gift and the evangelist gift is significant. The person with the gift of hospitality sees Christ in the stranger (see Matt. 25:35), and the evangelist visualizes the stranger "in Christ" (see Acts 8:26-40).

The church in North America today needs to put this gift to work. Our churches are declining, even in high population growth areas. Simultaneously, people who visit churches as they shop for a church home say that the main feature they seek is friendliness. Research in church growth and decline indicates that the number one reason people leave a particular church is a feeling of being unwanted, usually called the friendship factor. The gift of hospitality makes visitors know that they are wanted and needed. Visitors learn from these gifted persons that the gospel is good news for people, not a good subject for some program or product for an institution.

I want to share a discovery of this gift. A young woman who bought a new mobile home near a university was looking for a person to share the living quarters and monthly payments. After discovering her hospitality gift in a workshop I held in her church, she went to the church office and handed the pastor a key to her home. She said, "I've decided to keep my extra bedrooms open for persons you know in need of lodging. If you get a request for help for students' parents or friends or from persons visiting hospital patients, send them over. I'll be waiting." After I've announced a request for lodging for guests, persons with this gift usually come forth immediately with an offering of rooms.

Humor

A well-placed word or story of humor can bring peace to a troubled person or group. The definition of this gift is *the extraordinary ability to bring laughter and joy to situations and relationships to relieve tension, anxiety, or conflicts and to heal and free emotions needed for effective ministries.* Most of us know persons with this gift. Many of us have tried to develop it, since many good and humorous stories are available, but we have fallen on our faces. We buy the most recent joke and humorous quotation books and try to memorize them. Most of us fail in this attempt, but the gifted humorist rarely forgets a joke.

Persons with this gift never embarrass others with their jokes. They never make sport of ethnic persons. They do not delight in incorporating anything that is a putdown in their jests. They never force others to laugh at their humor. They never rely on references to private parts of the human anatomy as a means of lightening the mood of their hearts. They do not joke about illnesses, such as AIDS, drug and substance abusers, or deficiencies, such as handicapping conditions of mind and body. They do not stereotype people in their stories of humor.

Most of them are gifted with puns. They can create a "funny" from nearly every conversation, not as an attention getter but as a way to elevate moods. Their humor is often a means of correcting false information without embarrassing someone else. When they tell a well-known joke, it is always done with good taste and not to take the floor but to free the floor for wider participation. After a hearty laugh, most persons feel relaxed and free to speak about serious matters without irritation and restraints.

Humor appears in the Bible. Paul indulges in it in 1 Corinthians 12:12-24. We often overlook this and other biblical humor because of our bias that says religion must be a serious matter. But when we read Paul, as serious as he seems to be most of the time, we see much humor. Can you imagine a foot talking to a hand or an ear talking to an eye? Can you visualize the body as one huge eyeball? a large foot? an ear? Can you imagine the whole human being as one large liver? Well, that's the picture Paul paints for us in this scripture. It's funny, really funny! And Paul gets his point across. The party spirit of the Corinthians disappears after they all see how ludicrous they have been.

I see Paul's humor in Galatians 5:12. He was in a wrangle with some persons calling others back to the practice of circumcision. In the midst of this heated debate, Paul says in effect, "I wish they would make a slip and cut the whole thing off" (mutilation). Or "if they insist on flesh, cut it all off! Don't stop with a mere end piece."

I see a bit of humor in John 13:6-15. Jesus spends a lot of time, effort, and energy washing the disciples' dirty feet. He comes to Peter who resists, but our Lord warns him about the consequences. Peter retorts, "Don't stop with my feet. Wash my hands and my head. Wash me all over!" Then after it is all over, Jesus sits down and asks, "Now, tell me what I've just done!" Can't you hear these slow-learning disciples of our Lord saying, "Why, you've just washed our feet"? If they didn't respond this way, why did Jesus have to explain it?

I see humor in the incident regarding a lamp (see Mark 4:21). The light was no electric lamp or flashlight. It was an open candle. Can't you imagine the laughter Jesus got when he suggested that a burning candle certainly isn't appropriate under a mattress that could either put the light out or catch on fire? I can hear the laughter of his audience when he indicated that a lamp has no place under a bucket.

Another illustration of our Lord's use of humor is his statement of the obvious when he suggested that a person is smart about dangers if he or she is tipped off. He has fun with the householder who would have been standing ready for defensive action if he had known that a thief was coming (see Luke 12:39).

I submit that faith, facts, and fun are not mutually exclusive. Entertainment should be a significant part of religious expression, and it doesn't have to copy secular modes. We are feeling beings. God created us as beings who make most decisions according to how we feel about things—not what we know as facts. I often test this fact in my workshops by asking, "What is the most critical decision a person makes other than to become a follower of Christ?" Always, they answer, "Whom to marry." Then I ask, "How many of you made that decision based on facts or logic?" You guessed it. They all engage in what I call verification laughter. At this point, I share my favorite story. I asked a friend if he was in love, and he answered, "I don't know. The last time I felt like this I had hepatitis!" I think everyone who has fallen in love can identify with this feeling.

Humor is a means of blending, if not enhancing, facts with positive feelings. Humor is often a sacred opportunity to use emotions to transform harsh realities into manageable means of faith living. He who laughs well also lives well. Many persons have an extraordinary ability to help us laugh. Dick Van Dyke, the humorous actor, wrote *Faith, Hope, and Hilarity.* In that book he says that the basis for his humor as a Christian is this proverb: "A merry heart doeth good like a medicine." Worlds apart, but writing about the same subject, is Elton Trueblood. His book *The Humor of Christ* examines the hypothesis that many of Christ's teachings are either incomprehensible or indefensible if they cannot be understood as humor. While some humor is intended to ridicule or scold, most sets out to release souls from emotional prisons. Laughter is liberating. Trueblood is no humorist, but he certainly helps us to see that our Lord used a significant amount of humor to liberate us from error, confusion, and sin.

9

I Will Bless You to Be a Blessing

A part of Genesis 12:2 gives us an apt way of describing *charismata*, spiritual gifts. They are blessings to bless the church and to bless the world through the church. So we continue with a study of these blessings.

Intercessory Prayer

The Greek word for "intercessory prayer" is *enteuxis*, found in 1 Timothy 2:1 and 4:5. Other references appear in Gifts' Definitions and Biblical References, page 177. The word means "conference," "petition," a "bringing together," or "intervention on another's behalf."

The definition of this spiritual gift is *the extraordinary ability to know when, how, and for whom or what to pray with effective results*. I am not speaking of the general role of praying that belongs to every child of God, one based mainly on an intimate exchange between God and one's soul. This role of praying is as natural to faith as breathing is to life. But the gift of intercessory prayer is different. It is a special dimension of prayer that some persons have and some do not.

The ones with this ability characteristically feel and need to pray for another, others, or a situation and stick with it until they sense a release. Unlike the basic prayer activity of all Christians, intercessory praying persists until something happens. The gifted experience a special and somewhat exciting delight in praying for others, almost to the exclusion of their own needs. In early periods of Christian history, and to some extent today, such persons lived apart from others in meditation and contemplation. Their total lives became a prayerful ministry.

Today, these charismatic intercessors are prompted by a sense of the presence of God (Holy Spirit) who often reveals to them the special need to pray for others. They joyfully receive a special request for prayer, not only from God but also from others. Many receive flashes of insight or urgent feelings about certain people and feel a need to go to God in prayer on their behalf. Often, they have not thought of or been in touch with these persons for months or years. Suddenly, they have a strong spiritual urge to pray for them. They do not normally have a vision of any particular problem, but they "know that they know" the persons need their prayers. While other Christians occasionally have similar experiences, gifted intercessors find these occurrences to be normal.

Many intercessors have an accompanying prayer language that facilitates their intercession (see 1 Cor. 14:2). The language unknown to them helps in their intercessions because they do not always know why or for what to pray. They mentally concentrate or focus on the person or situation and let their spiritual language mechanism run freely. They always conclude such an intercession with an overwhelming sense of peaceful completion.

These persons usually respond quickly to prayer requests from the pulpit or other sources. Many of them call the pastor or other source for more details because they want to pray specifically and effectively for results.

To them, praying is a vital ministry and not idle words or nods in God's direction. It is work—meaningful, joyful work—designed to accomplish something. They do not delight so much in bringing God to act upon the needs of others as they do in bringing others and their needs into the presence of God. Many spiritually visualize taking their prayer subjects by the hand and accompanying them into the presence of God and remaining there until something changes. Praying and not giving up until something happens is hard work (see Luke 18:1).

A last aspect of this gift is the experience of completion or satisfaction after the hard work of prayer is done. Then they feel free to move on to something else. They have no need to spend any more energy on it. They have the power to leave it with God and to think of it no more.

A word of caution here. A local pastor may look for retired, homebound, and other available persons who are hindered from other active ministries to be prayer warriors or intercessors in prayer for the work of the church. The problem is that God doesn't always follow such a line of convenience or reasoning. God chooses the persons and the gifts. We never know the why, only the what. If the persons mentioned do not have the gift, they could easily burn out or turn sour on prayer. Without the gift, they do not have the necessary accompanying power of the Holy Spirit to operate it.

But who wants to resist the pastor asking for prayers? General praying is fine, but intercessory prayer is energy draining and may be of long duration. We damage persons when we recruit them to do something for which they are not suited, equipped, or called (see Rom. 11:29). We do everyone a spiritual service to take the time to find the right persons (the gifted) for the right ministry.

Interpretation

I realize that this gift should be next to the gift of tongues, but alphabetical listing does not permit this order. Yet, this gift of interpretation actually goes beyond translating *glossolalia*. The Greek word for "interpretation" is *diermeneuo*, meaning "to make clear," "to explain a message," "to expound on a meaning," "to translate into another language or vernacular for understanding." My definition of the gift is *the extraordinary ability to hear, comprehend, and translate spiritual messages given by others in unknown languages or to clarify spiritual messages from one who speaks in a known language, not known by the interpreter, to a functional vernacular.*

In many cases persons easily understood what a person of another known language was saying, but they did not know the language—had never heard or studied it. They only knew the essential spiritual message coming through. Others spoke in a language unknown to them but recognized by others as a bona fide language. The speakers did not know what they were saying, but others understood and received a vital message of spiritual value. Still others understood and revealed spiritual messages given by persons who spoke in an unknown tongue.

Interpretation is a gift of unfolding a mystery hidden in a foreign language or nonlanguage and also a vital ministry of expounding the

103

good news of Christ's redemption in a known language. An example of the latter is in Luke 24:27 that describes how Jesus interpreted the Old Testament scripture to the two disciples on the road to Emmaus. Without question, because of the problem of communication between persons today who even speak the same language, the church needs interpreters to elucidate the good news of Christ.

The gospel has been so strained, stretched, and twisted by distorters that the church is divided and rendered powerless in many places. By their political schemes, theological systems, and scientific principles, many persons take undue liberties with the message of God's love in Christ for the world. Only sound interpretation can deliver us from this evil. God has given this spiritual gift of interpretation to do just that.

Having said that, I do not want to skirt the matter of the classical need to have interpreters to clarify what is being said by people who speak in tongues, that is, the prayer and praise language millions enjoy. So that tongues might build up the body of Christ, Paul demanded an interpreter (see 1 Cor. 14:13, 26). Confusion has occurred, however, from an apparent clash between 1 Corinthians 12:10 and 14:13.

In 12:10, Paul uses "another" to individualize certain gifts. "Another" means another *one*, not all or the same. This gift of interpretation is given not to the same person with the gift of tongues but to another (one). Then in 14:13, Paul demands that the person who speaks in a tongue should pray for the power to interpret. On the surface, he seems to be contradicting himself.

My understanding is that Paul was trying to decrease the use of tongues, mainly because of a widespread abuse. One way to eliminate any further misuse was to make sure that one had the power to interpret before speaking in a tongue. Since God gives the gifts according to divine choice and will (12:11), Paul knew that interpretation would not be given in response to a request.

A gift (*charisma*) is a property of God's grace that cannot be earned or appropriated by any means, especially by prayer. Otherwise, it would be something other than a grace-gift. Therefore, without the gift or power to interpret, speaking in tongues is pointless. The principle is, no interpreter, no tongues. This principle would cut down on the confusion chapters 12-14 addressed. Paul did not say that if one prays for the power to interpret, the request would be granted. He was smarter than that. He was a brilliant logician and presenter of God's revealed wisdom. His readers were not too bright, in fact ignorant (12:1). The ignorant use of any gift is no better than having no gift at all.

Persons with this gift clearly hear a message that transcends the speaker's words, but it is never in conflict with the speaker's words. Whatever the message, it is never incompatible with other messages in the New Testament. The messages are not quotations of biblical passages. That would be redundant. God knows that a clear understanding of what the Bible says is what the Bible says and not some unknown tongue of a speaker. When they hear no distinct message from one speaking in tongues, the gifted are more likely to remain silent and aloof, especially if they suspect that their or the speaker's gift is not operating. The intent of interpretation is elucidation and assurance.

A question may arise here about the similarity of interpretation, prophecy, and wisdom. Prophecy is the power to receive a direct message from God for the moment and situation. Interpretation is the power to explain a situation or another person's words or actions. In this case, the situation may be the Bible. Prophecy, as an activity of studying biblical prophecies is more correctly the activity of an interpreter, not a person with the gift of prophecy.

Wisdom is the ability to decipher from grand, universal, and sacred principles what is reasonable and practical for the moment or situation. God built into the universe laws and principles, one of which is love. Everyone knows the presence and value of *agape* love, but many of us do not know how to live according to that kind of love. Wisdom is the gift that shows us that. Another example is communication. The gift of wisdom shows how effective communication can be accomplished.

I hope this explanation will arouse enough interest to motivate us to fine-tune our understanding of the gifts—how they differ and what they uniquely offer the church. The health of the body depends upon this understanding.

Knowledge

The Greek word for this gift is *gnosis*, meaning "to know universal and timeless truths and facts relating to God's will and the mission of the church." Not necessarily knowledge in the sense of acquired data, it is a knowing that may pertain to the natural world and order of things, but it has a special bias toward God's specific relationship to the church and its relationship to the world. It is a spiritual understanding of the universal scope of salvation for which the church is designed to be an agent (see 2 Cor. 5:18-19). The gift of knowledge is specifically mentioned in 1 Corinthians 12:8.

The definition of knowledge as a spiritual gift is the *extraordinary power to understand the universal and timeless truths of God and to link them with the church in its mission through Christ for justice and righteousness in the world.* Although every Christian has a general knowledge, imparted by the Holy Spirit, about the nature of Christ in relationship to the world (see 1 Cor. 2:12-16), God gives certain Christians an elevated level of understanding. It is an ability to bridge gaps between certain unavoidable realities: the gaps between religion and science, the spiritual and the material, and the historical biblical message and the modern mind.

This gift differs from the gift of discernment. Discernment, as already noted, is a special ability to ascertain intuitively and spiritually what is of God, of human nature, or of Satan. The gift of knowledge can be measured by reason, logic, and authority given by God. Probably the best example in scripture, other than Jesus Christ, is Paul (see 1 Cor. 8:1; 14:6). What we do not understand in some of Paul's writings is compensated for by the divine authority with which he writes. Even when we don't quite know what he is saying, we believe it anyway. The power of his knowledge and authority energizes our faith to trust him. Although we may not be able to follow the logic and reasoning of some gifted persons today, the Holy Spirit empowers us with trust and obedience (see 2 Tim. 1:13, 14).

Persons with this gift are prone to think and speak theologically. That is, they speak often with terms that link God and human life. "Theology" comes from two Greek words: *theos*, which is "God," and *logos*, which is "word" or "reason." Thus, the definition is "thinking and speaking intelligently of God-human relations." Of course, not only university and divinity school graduates have *gnosis*. Some of the greatest insights and truths about God come from persons with no formal higher education.

Also, speaking theologically does not mean quoting Bible verses. Most human beings with a mere educable amount of intelligence can memorize and relate certain Bible verses. The gift of knowledge is apparent when a person can relate the Bible verses to realities and living today. Knowledge does not take twentieth-century people back to first-century ways of living. It brings the universal and timeless truths as redemptive realities for living today. It translates the Jesus of history into the Christ of faith.

Persons with the spiritual gift of knowledge often speak with a ring of authority in what they say. They do so because they "know what they know," even though they know some truths are not easy to articulate. Speaking out of this gift, they don't need the approval of others to whom or for whom they speak. Many times, though, they appear to be dogmatic and highly opinionated. Consequently, unless they are tempered by other caring gifts, such as pastoring, mercy, exhortation, and helps, they may be quick to discount persons who reject the fruit of their knowledge.

Their insights frequently reach beyond biblical quotations, though never in conflict with the Bible, to morals and ethics based on eternal, universal, and timeless principles that embrace love and Christian servanthood. They easily distinguish between culturally derived and divinely designed principles for just and righteous living. Meanings and overtones are of greater importance than gathered facts and data. Doctrines based on sacred and timeless principles interest them more than those based on biblical words and events.

For example, they are more interested in why Jesus said to "do this in remembrance of me" (Luke 22:19) than the what or how of eating bread, drinking wine, and distributing them. Or their insight shows that the significance of baptism resides not in how much water is applied but in what timeless and universal truth the act conveys.

Another example of the gift of knowledge is one person's description of the Book of Revelation: "The book simply but profoundly means, 'Hang in there. Don't give up. All this has meaning and purpose. It will soon be clear and worth everything to you.'" With those few words, the person offering the description captured the entire meaning of that difficult book. But notice that the gift of knowledge does not show us how to hang in there. It is more inspirational and theoretical than practical. The gift of wisdom shows us how to hang in there. The gift of helps assists us in doing it, and exhortation offers us comfort and companionship along the way.

Leadership

The spiritual gift of "leadership" comes from the Greek *proistemi*. Its meaning suggests the position of a sailor who stands on the bow of a boat to point out the way to a destination and to guide the skipper around dangers in the way.

Translated into spiritual gift language, leadership leads, guides, or directs other members of the body of Christ to fulfill the church's commission. It also equips its recipients to offer effective guidance to individuals who yearn to be effective participants in the ministries of the church. Unlike the gift of teaching, a gift that can be used in hypothetical situations such as the classroom, leadership is a gift that instructs on location.

Today's sailors are trained first in the classroom. Then they go to a hands-on location. The instructor there is the *proistemi*, or leader. He or she stands on the bow of the boat, points out the direction, and shouts instructions to the crew related to directions and goals. The same is true with spiritual guidance.

This person has *an extraordinary ability to envision God's will and purpose for the church and to demonstrate persuasive skills to capture the imaginations, energies, skills, and spiritual gifts of others to pursue and accomplish God's will.* This individual has the ability to set goals for the body of Christ, to see what is essential for the well-being of all involved, and to motivate all in such a way that the body will enjoy harmony as it works to accomplish its goals. The biblical reference for this is Romans 12:8. Others appear in Gifts' Definitions and Biblical References.

Persons with the gift of leadership see goals and means for reaching them long before other church members do. The gifted often appear to have their heads in the clouds with their wistful thinking and grandiose schemes. They can describe how individuals can personally benefit spiritually, as well as the church and the kingdom. We are drawn to such persons because they never lose sight of the needs of the individual in the process toward the body's larger goal.

The leader is always out front, on the bow of the boat as it were, often pointing out ways that appear dangerous and impossible but only because the whole scene is in view. Leaders are quick to indicate weaknesses and dangers but in such a way that inspires, encourages, and challenges. Unlike persons with the gift of exhortation who inspire and encourage by being and doing with others, leaders stand at a distance. No member of the church is lonelier than the leader. The leader is often alone in dreams and visions, alone in seeing and specifying dangers, and alone in example. A large amount of faith and energy is required to operate this gift. Usually, the gifted leader has the gift of faith. Faith, which is a power of stick-to-itiveness is a stubborn belief in God and in individuals.

Often, these gifted persons say, "Just trust me. It's OK. It'll work. You'll see what I'm talking about as we move together along the way." And people follow! They can keep goals in focus even as they cultivate intimate relationships along the way. They demonstrate a divine ability to use group dynamics, although they may be untrained in the secularly offered training in leadership and management. Leaders develop skills of communication from self-motivation. They never dictate; their language rarely includes "oughts" and "shoulds."

In their use of the Bible, they tend to grasp broad principles more than specific rules, laws, and commands. Love and harmony are more vital than law and doctrine. They consider loving and caring services more important than "correct" rituals in corporate worship. Their understanding of theology and doctrine tends to focus on functions rather than form, on meaning rather than systems. To them, the ultimate realities of the faith are directly related to inner or intimate reality—a personal experience with Christ. This experience is a prologue for kingdom living and the eventual divine consummation of all things. That explains their extraordinary ability to relate individuals to one another without losing sight of specific and future goals.

Leaders are not good followers. God gifted them to lead, not to follow. And they are quick to volunteer to lead a project, even though they may not know anything about it at first. This tendency comes from their strong inclination to lead, no matter what.

Others often misunderstand their self-confidence to lead as conceit or egocentricity. Others often perceive them as power hungry. They may appear more visionary than practical and more futuristic than contemporary. But in the midst of opposition because of these perceived weaknesses, they display grace-filled tolerance and patience that win the day for them. Leaders view criticism as a benefit, not a challenge.

While leaders by nature and position are always ahead or out front, they never deliberately hold themselves aloof from followers and never consider themselves superior. *Rank* is not a favorite word with them. This attitude is one reason they often develop warm and close relations with the followers. They value honesty and integrity as they seek to follow their own advice. Leaders want to be trusted because they consider trustworthiness one of the highest virtues of Christian living. Other Christians follow gifted leaders, not because of any virtue of the leaders but because they discern the virtuous Christ in them.

Martyrdom

Christianity's history is full of examples of this powerful witness. That's what martyrdom is—a strong, if not stubborn, and open adherence to faith in Christ and obedience to his will. The gift of faith usually accompanies the gift of martyrdom.

The word comes from the Greek *martureo*, which means "to bear witness," or *sunepimartureo*, which means "to confirm." We associate death with the words because in early Christianity it meant death to be accused of being a Christian. Stephen was the first New Testament example (see Acts 7:54-60). But the initial attestation was the ultimate confirmation of a divine love expressed in John 3:16. It is one thing to say how much one loves and believes; it is another to confirm that love and that belief in the midst of opposition and hardship with death. The life and death of Jesus Christ offers us an example. Others followed Christ and gave their lives for the faith as well.

Martyrdom, however, does not necessarily entail death. Sometimes it would be easier and far more noble to die than to live. And this gift does not always mean witnessing in the face of hardships and serious threats. It could mean a stubborn persistence in the midst of boring circumstances or extreme indifference. Sometimes it is harder to be passively ignored than to be violently rejected.

Thus, our definition of the gift of martyrdom is *the extraordinary ability to stand firm on divinely inspired convictions and divinely di-rected ministries without equivocation or self-aggrandizement.* Scriptural references appear in Gifts' Definitions and Biblical References. This gift is not the evangelistic witness designed and empowered by the Holy Spirit to win others to Christ (see "Evangelism" entry). It is more a confession, which is a statement of an intimate experience of divine reality, than the use of words to communicate objective facts. Paul captures the true witness in 1 Corinthians 12:3 when he says, "No one can say 'Jesus is Lord' except by the Holy Spirit."

Several characteristics appear in the demeanor and verbal witness of persons with this gift. One is stubbornness, which is an unyielding position of faith and practice. I often have fun with persons who score high on this gift. At first, they and their spouses think only of dying—not a pleasant thought. Then, after I have explained other dimensions, such as inflexibility, intractability, obduracy, or stubbornness, many spouses smile and nod their heads in full agreement with the description.

Hearing of torture and murder some Christians willingly suffer moves us deeply. Learning how frequently these events occur in today's world is often incomprehensible, especially in light of facts stating they happen more frequently today than in most earlier periods of our history. But we know of many, many more who are not blessed by a quick death. They suffer long for their faith. They must go on living day by day, and some must endure a lifetime under painful and trying pressures that come from their faith in Christ. Yet, they live with joy and special strength as they persist in their faith. Their gift is the power to endure hardships so that others may be strengthened and encouraged to stand firm in Christian faith and service.

They are single-minded in their service because they believe they live under divine guidance and care. Their experience of joy overcomes temptations to complain. Their hope and vision offer reasons for endurance. They think of dying in terms of "for" something rather than "because" or "from" something. For the most part, their thoughts focus on what they are living "for" and not "with." They do not tend to withdraw from tough and threatening situations. They willingly give themselves as examples of perseverance.

I must add something about the value of, perhaps, less dramatic martyrdoms in the local church and community. This witness will never make headlines in secular and religious newspapers and certainly not a new edition of *Foxe's Book of Martyrs*. Nevertheless, such tenacious and resolved persons keep the fires of faith, hope, and love alive in the local church. Without much effort, most of us can name some of them. We know their steady and unyielding love for Christ and the church, their willingness to be overworked and their readiness to be overlooked, and their faithfulness in abuse as well as in use. Their witness is not so much to convert others to the faith as it is to demonstrate a personal relationship with the Christ who gives faith. Their witness is never, "Look at me and what is happening to me!" but, "Praise God from whom all blessings flow!"

10

Having Gifts That Differ

We're not the same. We're different. And because we are, every Christian is interesting and challenging. One facet of Christian living that gives rise to differences is the spiritual gift (*charisma*). Differences, though, do not make one superior—just functionally different to serve specific needs of the body of Christ, the church. For example, the gift of leadership is not to operate as the gift of administration or vice versa. Also, if one has a combination of mercy, hospitality, and teaching, that person's spiritual disposition and temperament will be different from another whose gift-mix includes exhortation, martyrdom, and evangelism.

These two mixtures are as different in the body of Christ as the muscular and the vascular systems are in the human body. Yet, both serve the same body with the same objective—vital life. Finding many persons with the same spiritual disposition is rare because most have different gift-mixes and all gifts differ in function. Too, each gift, from one person to another, may vary in quantity and quality. These degrees of differences and functions determine spiritual temperament, which also affects one's personality. Paul's summary statement in his prologue to the gifts in Romans 12:6, "Having gifts that differ . . . ," is a profound affirmation of essential differences. So we continue our survey of differing gifts.

Mercy

As it is with all gifts (*charismata*), all Christians have a measure of mercy, but certain ones receive the special spiritual gift of *eleeo*—the *extraordinary ability to feel and to act upon genuine empathy for others who suffer distressing physical, mental, emotional, social, and spiritual pain*. The "acting upon" is an attempt to relieve the sufferer of distress, pain, or discomfort.

Mercy is a supersensitive ability that causes the gifted to feel the discomfort of the sufferer. It is a feeling with and for a person in misery that demands an act to relieve both the person in distress and the person with the gift of mercy. *Eleeo* also describes God's loving and redeeming acts toward the undeserving, initially toward Israel and eventually toward the whole world (see John 3:16; 2 Cor. 5:19). In the body of Christ, the church, it translates into joyful acts that reflect Christ's compassion for the church and, through the church, the world.

This gift is the only one that is the subject of a beatitude: "Blessed are the merciful, for they shall obtain mercy" (Matt. 5:7). The persons with the gift of mercy identify so intimately with distressed persons that the only way they can be relieved is by relieving the distressed. This does not mean a self-aggrandizing element is in the use of this gift. It simply means that this gift, as all gifts, has a certain vulnerability with it. For example, the teacher *has to* teach, the leader *has to* lead, and the evangelist *has to* win others to Christ to be fulfilled. Rarely do we accuse teachers who *have to* teach, encouragers who *have to* inspire, or evangelists who *have to* convert of self-serving. Is it fair, then, to accuse others with the gift of mercy of self-serving if they *have to* try to relieve others of pain?

God's love and compassion are so real to God that only effective redemption for humans can deliver God from the distress of *agape* vulnerability. That God suffers "with" and not just "for" is the heart of incarnation. Yet, God *has to* love with a self-emptying procedure because it is the nature of God to do so.

Church members with the gift of mercy have peculiar behavioral traits. They cannot bear the thoughts of administering pain to others, even in the process of relieving others of pain. When administering the gift presents pain to another, the gifted apologize profusely. Good examples are nurses who must use needles and dentists who have to drill.

I hope we can see the difference between this gift and the gifts of helps and service. Helps is strictly person-centered or other-centered. Helps objectively identifies the needs of persons and gets on with helping. Service identifies the same objective needs but is motivated to act by a sense of the presence of God, meaning that the act of servicing another's needs is actually an act of worshiping God. It is God-centered. The gift of mercy operates from the yearning to reduce discomfort, distress, or pain—not only for the sufferer but also for the gifted. Thus, the gift is condition-centered. Because of these different motives, behavioral traits differ, too.

The merciful can be identified by their behavior while watching a drama that portrays suffering. They squirm and become tense when they see others hurting. In actual life, they act immediately to relieve others of hurt, whether emotional or physical.

Because they often appear to be so sympathetic, they may be victims of others who use their plight to manipulate for attention. However, God apparently built into this gift a special sensitivity to detect insincere motives or counterfeit misery. The gifted have the ability to detect false misery or self-imposed pain and easily withdraw their feelings. When they recognize authentic suffering, they withhold nothing to operate the gift fully.

They do not consider the worthiness of others in real distress. Their interest, though, leans more toward unhealthy or hurting people than healthy ones. This focus on pain and suffering also motivates them to work for the elimination of conditions that cause illness and misery. Many find their way into social movements and professions in social services that concentrate on eliminating conditions that cause suffering. Reducing the threat of conditions also reduces the prospects of the gifted's pain or suffering. In fact, many mercy-gifted Christians look for persons who suffer or conditions that cause distress to occupy their divinely given energy. A word of caution is necessary at this point.

Two severe abuses of this gift come from getting out of step with Christ, which is a possibility for all gifts. One is to enjoy helping the unhealthy or distressed so much that the value of the healthy is totally overlooked and unappreciated. The other abuse is that the gifted create pain and suffering when they cannot find someone in distress or pain. Some people are not happy unless others are unhappy. When there is no apparent need for rescue operations, they create conditions that cause suffering. Then they are the first to the rescue!

Let's get back to the positive. Cheerfulness and compassion are dominant traits of the merciful. Seldom do they speak with doom and gloom. Even less frequently do they criticize hurting persons. They characteristically delight in touching hurting persons, and their language is always encouraging.

No gift is designed to work exclusively outside the body of Christ. Yet, many gifts are forced to operate in secular situations almost exclusively because of the church's ignorance or disinterest. So, when the church does not provide opportunities for certain gifts to be used within, the gifted with mercy can serve the body well as catalysts who call the church's attention to opportunities to relieve the suffering and debilitating conditions of others outside.

Miracles

I know! Miracles were supposed to have ceased during the period of the early church, the first century, but they didn't. God has ways of correcting our misunderstandings and ignorance when we are open to God. Miracles happen today. And do you know where we find the largest number of and most dramatic miracles? In medical, social, and educational fields. Rarely in the churches are they recognized and acknowledged.

We can easily get sidetracked concerning miracles. Before the coming of the industrial age, scientific and technological revolution, interplanetary travel, and the computer age, everything out of the ordinary was considered a miracle. A miracle was anything that could not be explained or caused by natural laws. We may be tempted to think that with all the advances in science and technology there is no need for the church to consider the miraculous. Let's revisit it anyway.

"Miracle" is a dubious English translation of two Greek words, *energemata dunameon*, which respectively and more correctly produce in English "energies" and "power." *Energemata* can also be translated "operations" in English. Rather than continue to use the misunderstood "miracle" for this *charisma*, I think we would understand it better as "powerful operation" or "powerful works." It is not beyond our ability to recognize persons used mightily by God to do things that others could not do.

The main biblical reference to this spiritual gift is 1 Corinthians 12:10, and there are many more. I list them in the Gifts' Definitions and Biblical References. The definition is *the extraordinary ability God gives to some persons to do powerful works that transcend other gifts and our perception of natural laws and means.*

We are not clear just how this gift relates to other gifts that we too often consider spectacular, such as healings and exorcism. Actually, all gifts are spectacular since they operate only out of the power of the Holy Spirit, a force unavailable from natural laws. One reason for this lack of clarity is that more often than not, long after the event of the "powerful operation," we recognize it as something extraordinary. But to a significant degree, we see certain characteristics among those through whom this powerful energy flows to do great works for the church and the world through the church.

Some characteristics resemble the operation of the gift of faith but with a slight difference in the lack of intentionality. The person who obviously has this gift does not necessarily know what is happening. He or she does what is prompted by an inner stirring of the Holy Spirit, and something eventually comes to light as extraordinary. It is unlike teaching because the teacher knows that he or she is teaching, unlike encouraging because the exhorter knows that exhortation is being worked, or unlike healing because the healer knows that healing is being attempted. The miracle worker does not have the luxury of this intentionality, except a strange inclination to be loyal to a prompting.

The person gifted with this powerful energy does not say, "Now I am going to perform a miracle. Stand back and behold!" The gifted are often surprised by the outcome of their active response to a prompted need. A good illustration is the persistent inclination two aged women had to pray for D. L. Moody, the world-famous evangelist, without knowing why they should pray for such an effective preacher. One day, something strongly moved Mr. Moody to find a place of prayer while walking down a street in New York City. He went to a house and asked for a private room. There and then he became endowed with a new power that increased his influence to win thousands to Christ. Although he preached the same sermons and gave the same invitations, something extraordinary increased the effectiveness of all that he did in ministry. Someone traced transformations of certain individuals who became renowned spiritual leaders, right down to Billy Graham, as a result of what happened later in one of Moody's services in England. This outcome is nothing short of a miracle. Intercessory prayer? Maybe. Faith? Possibly. Powerful operation? Definitely.

Characterizing the gift of powerful operation is not easy. One trait is the lack of repeatability. Unlike the teacher, administrator, leader, encourager, prophet, and others with rather predictable behaviors and results, a person chosen by God to be a channel of extraordinary power rarely knows when something is happening. Only sometimes does the person know of a strong inner prompting. Biblical accounts of miracles bear this out. Take a look at the plagues brought on Egypt. Though their occurrence was a powerful operation, it has not been repeated. Look at the feeding and watering of the band of Israelites in the wilderness. Except for well drillers who work with their sharp drills, hammers, and pumps people don't usually claim striking rocks for water as a calling. Even dowsers don't claim to produce water; they just locate it.

Consider our Lord's turning water into wine. It did not set into motion a ministry of wine making. It was a one-time event. Consider Paul's instrumentality for blinding a magician (see Acts 13:11). Thank God that blinding spiritual reprobates did not become a calling for some. We could cite scores of spectacular events inside and outside the Bible and still not come up with a specific pattern for powerful works. Yet, we know they happen, and we rarely anticipate them.

Therefore, we must be open to the One whose presence always brings marvelous surprises. The most likely candidates for channeling God's miraculous power could be those who willingly and faithfully operate their known and predictable spiritual gifts. They are already conditioned and committed to be channels of God's grace. It is my prayer that all members of the body of Christ will maintain a level of consciousness toward being a possible conduit of God's marvelous grace, the energizing power of the Holy Spirit.

Amazing advances are being made in science and technology. I do not believe all is of God; most stems from pure human intelligence and an openness to possibilities. I believe the counterpart is possible in the realm of the spiritual. Whatever the limitation here, it is of our own lack of application and openness to God's spirit. I believe the world is disappointed in Christianity mainly because of our timidity and fear in the face of extraordinary possibilities. I do not believe God's power is inferior to whatever produces weapons that wound and kill and ideologies that cause us to hate. I believe for every weapon and means that negate human worth and contaminate hope for quality living, there is a miracle, a powerful work, available to God's faithful people. Paul said, "Hence I remind you to rekindle the gift of God that is within you . . . for God did not give us a spirit of timidity but a spirit of power" (2 Tim. 1:6-7).

Missionary

Without question, evidence points to certain members of the church who have an *extraordinary ability to cross over the boundaries of race, color, creed, language, geography, culture, and subcultures to serve the physical, psychological, social, and spiritual needs of neglected peoples.* This gift is different from *apostolos*, which is a specialized gift that empowers persons to herald the good news of Christ and to organize converts into effective communities of faith. Both, apostles and missionaries, are different from *euagelistes* (evangelists), who have special abilities that win others to Christ.

All missionaries are not apostles, and all apostles are not missionaries. All evangelists are not missionaries or apostles, and all missionaries and apostles are not evangelists. But some of each may be each of the others. So who are missionaries?

They are gifted with the ability to cross boundaries that often divide the human family. They carry various and sundry gifts, skills, and interests. Some of these are not particularly identified as spiritual gifts, but they are most definitely human, social, and technical skills that translate God's love and grace into deeds supplying basic human needs.

Missionaries may be medical specialists (for human beings and for animals), doctors and nurses, lawyers, economists, industrial engineers, dentists or dental technicians, teachers of basic human skills, or agronomists. They may be foresters, carpenters, plumbers, electricians, civil engineers, road builders, or dietitians. They may be Bible teachers or evangelists.

The essence of their gift is not so much their skill or other spiritual gift as their Holy Spirit–energized yearning and extraordinary ability to cross boundaries and joyfully adjust to new and different peoples and circumstances. Their main technology is relating to differing others with a contagious warmth that radiates the love of Christ.

To a great degree, this gift resembles some of the others, such as helps, service, hospitality, leadership, administration, exhortation, and healing. The gift of missionary may be an addition to one or more of the other gifts. Whatever the case, certain behavioral traits identify the gift.

These persons have an inner desire and dream of aiding others in another land or culture. They are visionary in that they believe they can make a difference in the lives of others. Whenever missions is mentioned or promoted in their local church, something stirs within and they respond accordingly. They learn, though, that sending money and other supplies, even other persons, does not silence their inner mission voice. Individuals who respond bodily by going to the mission field learn quickly whether that voice was of God and the gift or some emotion attached to a temporary feeling.

Persons with the missionary gift usually stay missionaries for a lifetime. Unfortunately, some who return after a minimum term feel they must justify their actions by explaining that they can serve their calling better at home. They could receive inner peace by admitting their going into the field was an error and by discovering and operating their true gift. Missionary giving at home could possibly be a specialized form of the gift of giving (see Rom. 12:8). One can be greatly interested in the missions of the church without having the gift of missionary. Such could be helps, service, encouraging, even leadership or administration. It could be teaching, prophecy, knowledge, or wisdom. But the authentic gift of missionary cannot be satisfied with being a missionary in spirit at home. He or she must go physically, which means bodily.

Mission ministries are in decline in most mainline churches. Possibly two reasons account for this decline. One is that the church, in general, has been so effective in its former missions that the faith is now producing roots and fruit among the people served. God is raising indigenous servants of Christ, thus reducing our need to send people from this country.

Another explanation may not be as complimentary. Not too long ago, a popular teaching asserted, "We don't *have* missions; we *are in* mission." Then it went on to explain that each Christian is a missionary in his or her own right. This new philosophy or theology of missions described everyone as being in mission to one's neighbor. To be sure, the intent of this new emphasis attempted to put everyone in touch with missions, but what happened was a reduction of much of the church's former focus on foreign missions. This emphasis was indistinguishable from the prevailing ignorance about the spiritual gifts that renders the body of Christ ineffective. The unfortunate message from that lack of spiritual knowledge declared all are teachers, all are evangelists, all are helpers, all are leaders, all are administrators, all are healers, all are encouragers, and so on. We are everything generally and very little in particular. If everyone is a missionary and in mission, how can we excite the imagination of persons gifted as missionaries to fulfill Matthew 28:19-20?

Let us not allow the rise of native or indigenous servants of Christ among certain peoples of the world to blind and deafen us until we fail to see and hear the call of the millions of people the church has not yet reached for Christ. Let us not fail to remind the ones with other spiritual gifts that the world is still our parish.

Pastor

The Greek for "pastor" is *poimen*, meaning "shepherd." The word means "to protect," "to oversee," "to manage," "to care for," "to assemble," and "to feed." The definition of the gift is *the extraordinary ability to carry varieties of spiritual, physical, and social concerns for groups and individuals and to persist over long periods of time and circumstances with effective care-giving.* Biblical references appear in Gifts' Definitions and Biblical References.

Pastor is not one of the offices noted in the New Testament, such as deacon, elder, presbyter, and bishop; yet, in nearly every modern church a pastor is a titular official. The fact is that a person may be one of the officers mentioned, yet not have the *charisma* (spiritual gift) of pastoring (see Eph. 4:11).

The behavioral traits of the gift are akin to the responsibilities of a herdsman in the Old Testament and a shepherd in the New Testament. The person oversees not only individuals and their spiritual welfare but also the group (herd or flock) formed by the individuals in relationships. It is tempting to think that one may be trained in a seminary or in management seminars to be a pastor. But without the energizing power of the Holy Spirit, which makes it a *charisma*, pastor is merely a titular office, not a grace force that builds up the body of Christ (see Eph. 4:11-12, 16).

The spiritual gift of pastor carries the drive and capacity to shoulder concern for many people at one time, perhaps a class or an organization of youth, women, or men. It tends to be concerned about spiritual and physical needs related to maturation and effective participation in the body of Christ. The pastor responds to a call for help but also seeks to get others involved in the helping. To the gifted pastor, ministering is not a solo act; it is a flock or fold affair but never at the expense of confidentiality and privacy. Keenly aware of the value of healthy relations between people, she or he often acts parentally in managing relationships between the members.

The pastor knows that problems are inevitable and plans for their eventuality. Often, if problems do not come to one's attention, the pastor may look for them. The problems have to be there because that's the way life is. Once shepherds find the problems, they find fulfillment in negotiating them and seek to engage the whole flock in the joyful ministry. They enjoy group dynamics and often like to be with groups more than the individuals who make up the group. Pastors can spot bellwether members (sheep that lead) who can aid them in the ministries. A part of pastoral knowledge is that members will often follow other members (bellwether) more quickly than the appointed leader.

The pastor studies hard to apply the good news of Christ to the flock's needs. The pastor knows that Christ is *the* Good Shepherd, and that the membership tender is an undershepherd (see 1 Pet. 5:4). Those with the gift of pastor tend to teach or preach peace, harmony, cohesion, unity, purpose, common goals, and fellowship, the principle being, united we stand, divided we fall. Encountering a strayed member, the gifted shepherd is likely to say, "We have been missing you," or "We certainly do need you," or "What can we do to get you back?"

Another characteristic of this gift is to count members of whatever group, class, or church he or she serves. This way one can keep track of losses, something a shepherd fears keenly. Also, regard for growth and maturity is paramount to a shepherd. Numerical growth and relational growth indicate a shepherd's performance, an accounting for which the pastor must give to Christ.

I have discovered that many church school teachers are really pastors. They do not take instruction lightly, but their main interest is spiritual formation and group relationships. When members do not attend, these teachers (really pastors) attempt to get in touch with them during the week. Authentic teachers, as a rule, focus on well-prepared lessons and the students present, not the absentees. They prefer spending their available time during the week getting ready for persons inclined to attend. The pastor prefers relating and overseeing a wider spectrum of concerns than mere lessons.

I've noticed the same patterns among ordained ministers. The ones with the gift of teaching devote more weekly time to reading and studying to instruct their people on Sunday than to pastoral visiting. On the other hand, ordained ministers with the gift of pastoring devote more time to making meaningful contacts during the week than to preparing sermons. They are likely to wait until late in the week (probably Saturday night) to work on a sermon. This way, they have accumulated many concerns and needs from their parish visits, which feed them ideas for applicable sermons. These examples illustrate how different gifts motivate different ministries to the body of Christ.

Prayer-Praise Language

I choose to call speaking or praying in tongues a prayer-praise language. In my survey of hundreds of persons with the gift of *glossolalia*, or tongues, its use is more a prayer for praising God than anything else. Only a few indicated they use tongues for intercessory prayers or prayers for healing. Persons who believe they have the gift of healing use tongues for healing purposes. Others use it as a form of meditation, something by which they can free the mind of structured sentences and words that often restrict spiritual activity.

Glossolalia is a combination of two Greek words: *lalia*, signifying an utterance of sound, whether known or unknown as a language, and *glossa*, meaning literally "tongue" but implying something done with the human tongue that purports to be a language. *Glossolalia*, as a word, does not appear in the New Testament but has come to be a compound word that describes the phenomenon of tongues Paul writes about in 1 Corinthians 12–14. Biblical references may be found in Gifts' Definitions and Biblical References.

My definition of this spiritual gift is the *extraordinary ability to pray to and to praise God with beneficial wordless phrases or utterances not familiar to known languages, and with such a joy-filled intimacy with Christ that faith is strengthened and ministries become effective.* Most people know how controversial and confusing this gift has been and how this aspect has been one of the most troublesome of charismatism. That was the case with the primitive church, and it is no less true today.

I do not care to add to the debate over this gift. There are more books and pamphlets on the subject than the church deserves, and I do not intend to add another one. We cannot, however, overlook the experience that millions have with this gift today. I simply want to join Paul in acknowledging his experience (see 1 Cor. 14:13-16) and to evaluate its beneficial contributions.

Speaking in tongues is not original with Christians. A psychological phenomenon recorded in the history of pagan religions and cultic practices resembles what we're talking about. It is an emotional high that some reached during cultic dances and self-imposed trances. Most people considered this state to be esoteric and elitist because only highly disciplined persons could attain it. Many looked upon these persons as spiritual "stars," a counterpart of high achievers in physical athletics. It became a controversial item in primitive and recent Christianity not because of its psychological or social value but because of its abuses. That was why Paul wrote about it in three chapters of 1 Corinthians.

Paul never denied the presence of this gift, but he stringently criticized its abuse. It was apparent then as it is today that some spiritually strut their gifts. In Corinth the "tongues" persons belittled others as not being Christian if they did not have this language. A counter-accusation from the Praise-the-Lorders was that they were probably profaning our Lord in such gibberish (see 1 Cor. 12:3). Paul stepped into the center of the emotional arena and declared both sides right and wrong.

To the glossolalists, he said, "Haven't you heard your sisters and brothers across the aisle declare Jesus is Lord? Well, no one can say 'Jesus is Lord' except by the Holy Spirit." Then to the Praise-the-Lorders who accused the glossolalists of profaning Jesus in their gibber-jabber, Paul said, "No one speaking by the Spirit of God ever says 'Jesus be cursed'" (1 Cor. 12:3). In essence, Paul said, "You're both right, and you're both wrong. Now let me explain what I mean." Then he launched into his explanation of the varieties of gifts, their services, applications, results—all under the management of "the same Spirit . . . the same Lord . . . the same God" (12:4-6).

To be sure, no less confusion and misunderstandings about glossolalia exist today, but among the genuine Christians I have encountered and studied, positive traits produce good fruit. After all, Jesus said, "You will know them by their fruits" (Matt. 7:16). What follows is a description of this experience that falls outside the churches that require speaking in tongues as the only valid manifestation of the baptism of the Holy Spirit.

These grace-gifted people have a very real and active prayer life. They are inclined to pray aloud, which involves the entire body. Psychotherapists are now saying that there is healing value in making positive statements out loud about oneself and others. Stress-related diseases can be made worse by negative thoughts and statements. Most people I know with the prayer-praise gift seem to have less stress-related ailments and seem to maintain positive feelings about God and others. They pray with a vision of healing and wholeness. They have already worked through prayers of confession and contrition. These cannot be done with glossolalia, an unknown tongue.

They usually begin praying in their own language, at which time negatives are negotiated, and then they move into a high level of prayer with sounds familiar to them but unintelligible as a language. They find this form of praying effortless with a joyful flow unrestricted by syntax and definitions. There is no stammering or sighing, and they really feel intimately in touch with God.

Genuine prayer-praise language is personal and individual, that is, not copied from or set by the pattern of others. It cannot be taught. Because it is something so personal, we should never question its value for persons who have it. Whatever value they assign to it should not be judged by others, except in its abuse. They do not report a trance or highly emotional aberration, but they give witness to a profound sense of being in the presence of God. They never lose control of their senses and feelings, nor do they feel delivered into the control of the Holy Spirit. They do not have the experience referred to as being slain in the Spirit.

They do not describe their prayer language as the Spirit praying or speaking for or through them. It is something not from the outside in but from the inside out. It is an awe-inspiring experience of having the ability to participate fully in the Spirit so that a special ministry may be performed. They do not always know the content of what they say in their prayer and praise, but they know the joy of not being restricted by a learned language and thought pattern. Their communication with God is not dictated by word values and meanings given to them by others through a learned language. To them, God is beyond the control of all known languages and cannot be reduced to any one of them, even something unknown.

Some of them, nevertheless, eventually recognize a pattern of sounds in their utterances but do not let it become another language to restrict them. Most of them are not curious about what they may be saying or praying; they simply feel a great sense of trust in the physical act of mental freedom. Many claim that their initial event was the most transforming and peace-producing spiritual experience they've ever had. Eventually, as they matured, they discovered that the gift has two dimensions. One is a spiritual and psychological preparation for the other dimension, which is to become extraordinarily effective in ministry to others. The initial phase releases pent-up emotions and anxieties to free them to be fully effective in their caring and sharing with others. Many describe healings of emotional and related physical conditions that crippled their personality and their desire and need to help others.

In their relations with others, the gift is an aid to loving others unselfishly. Their religious convictions are strengthened and often revitalized. Their praying to God becomes more giving praise than petitioning for something. And when they offer petitional prayers they find more joy in praying for others than for themselves.

Because of misunderstandings and abuses of this gift, I feel the necessity to offer some cautions. During the course of my workshops, more questions are raised about abuses of than the value of the prayer-praise language gift. The greater value would be in describing the beneficial attributes of the gift. I hope the following will do as much for the users as the inquirers.

One prominent abuse is projection, that is, trying to convince others that this gift is for them, too. Sometimes persons ask, "Don't you want everything God has to offer?" This stock question is a put-down and a gross misunderstanding of *charismata*. Paul said, "To another [this means another *one*, and not *all*] various kinds of tongues" (1 Cor. 12:10). Also check the next verse:

> *All* these [the gifts] are inspired [more properly translated "energized" or "empowered"] by one and the same Spirit [meaning the same Spirit who empowers the other gift], who apportions [distributes] to each one [person] individually [not collectively or corporately] as he [namely, God or Spirit] wills [designs].
>
> —1 Corinthians 12:11, emphasis mine

To tell or to encourage another to seek a special gift that one has and enjoys is an abuse called projection.

Another abuse is to attribute the use of a gift to the Holy Spirit. Although the Spirit distributes and empowers the gift, it is absolutely up to the recipient of the gift to *use* it. Nowhere does the New Testament state that the Spirit does the speaking. In every case it says, "And they [the gifted] spoke in tongues."

A third abuse is to divide the body of Christ over the use of a gift. When this happens, the burden rests on the user. All gifts are to edify (build up), never to divide and tear down (see Eph. 4:12-14). The use of tongues has divided many churches. When this happens, our Lord certainly has no part in it. Satan is an artistic counterfeiter. A false gift can do nothing but hurt the body.

Guiding questions about the value and authenticity of the gift are as follows: Does it increase one's patience and love toward others? Does it leave one feeling closer to Christ? Does it cause one to look up, straight across, or down to others? Does its use cause one to feel superior or extra special in God's family? Does one feel compelled to use it despite resistance from or needs of others? Does one ever use it as a shorthand or an easy way of praying? Does one feel addicted to its use, that is, one cannot pray without it? Does one feel it is necessary to tell everyone about the gift? Can one be away from others who use it aloud without having great discomfort? Does one have to be in the presence of others when using the gift? Is there shame or timidity associated with its use? Is there a guilt feeling over its use or lack of use?

11

Rekindle the Gift

Just before beginning this chapter, I had to rekindle a fire in my fireplace insert. As I stirred the ashes, I found some coals hot enough to start another fire without having to use a match. So I placed some paper and wood on top and fanned for a flame. It worked!

Paul exhorts his young protégé to refire his gift for ministry. He reminds Timothy to fan the flame of the *charisma* "of God" (2 Tim. 1:6). I take this to mean that it is possible for us to lose power, but not the gift. According to Romans 11:29, the gift is "irrevocable," but that does not indicate it can't lose its power. Stirring or rekindling suggests effort required to get it going again. We do not choose our gifts, but we do choose whether to use them. So let's stir! Let's fan the flame! Let's rekindle the gift whose power resides in its use! You just may have the gift of prophecy. Let's take a look!

Prophecy

The Greek word for "prophecy" is *propheteia*. It means "revealing, manifesting, showing forth, making known, divulging, speaking out, or announcing vital information necessary for spiritual living and development." The definition of the spiritual gift is *the extraordinary ability to link biblical truths with God's will for today's living and to be an instrument for revealing or interpreting previous or current messages from God for righteous and just living in today's world.* The basic scriptural references to prophecy are 1 Corinthians 12:10, 29 and Ephesians 4:11—others may be found in Gifts' Definitions and Biblical References.

Paul emphasizes the significance of prophecy but not the kind we hear about so often. Prophecy may or may not contain a prediction of future events, but many of us have been conditioned to think of it only as an utterance about future events. Some think of it as only a biblical theme that predicts what is happening today and shall happen in the future. Both emphases overlook the dynamic reality of God's presence *now* and what God may want us to know *now* that may not be covered in scripture, except in dubious interpretations. Today's true prophets have the extraordinary ability to receive and to articulate current messages from God, positive as well as negative, for today's living.

The definition I've presented includes a statement about biblical truths. That is, today's prophecy will be consistent with the general principles of the Bible: the sovereignty of God, the never-failing love of God, the need for salvation found only in Christ, and living and relating to others according to the teachings and example of Jesus Christ. The gift of prophecy is not the academic or literary ability to sift out Old Testament predictions of New Testament occurrences and New Testament predictions of today's or future events. Anyone can study these passages with an adequate ability to read, remember, and use imagination. Usually, this study is conducted under the heading of biblical prophecy.

Authentic prophecy is revelational and *forth*telling, not *fore*telling. The prophets of the Old Testament and New Testament were not map or chart makers of the future but channels for God's immediate message to the people of that day and time and place. They were relevant. Their message from God was pertinent to the needs or conditions of the people. The same is true of authentic prophecy today. As it is with other gifts, the *charisma* of prophecy has unique traits.

The gifted persons are usually articulate. Similar to those with discernment, they can quickly spot the character and motives of people and can identify righteousness and unrighteousness, justice and injustice. As it is with persons having the gift of mercy, they easily identify with the victims of injustice or social ignorance. They are usually willing to experience personal brokenness to understand and to demonstrate the brokenness of others. Persons gifted with mercy attempt to extract someone's suffering, but prophets concentrate on the condition that causes a person's suffering. To cure or correct the condition relieves a sufferer and the prospects of suffering for many, many more persons. Also, prophets can see that suffering is not always the direct result of evil. Suffering can be used by God (see 2 Cor. 4:7-12).

Normally, they have a broad view of God's kingdom and righteousness, covering all life, not just spiritual concerns. Others may judge their focus on rights and wrongs as dogmatic and stubborn. Their emphasis is often on making decisions based on what they "know from God" rather than the slow process of education and spiritual growth. They dwell mainly in the emerging "now" but rarely without a hint of what "now" promises the future. Their bold and strict standards for behavior may hinder intimate and personal relationships. A strong sense of urgency impels them to call for a response to their pronouncements. They tend to be extremely restless while decisions and responses linger. They often feel that play is unimportant, even wrong, until people receive and act on God's revealed truths. A work ethic is important to them. They are usually results-directed rather than process-oriented persons. This characteristic distinguishes prophecy from exhortation: the latter's key is process.

Conditions are uppermost in prophets' thinking, though not without compassion for victims of conditions. In fact, compassion is their basic motivation—compassion for God's purpose and will and compassion for people broken by the rejection of God's will.

Theologically, they tend to be mystically current in the application of biblical truths. Their interest in biblical content is not so much historical as it is relevant for contemporary living and problems. Their understanding of eschatology is that now, the current moment, is always the fulfilling moment of divine truth. The end is always the here and now, and so is the beginning. Today is no temporary bridge between yesterday and tomorrow. Today is all there is or ever was or ever shall be. Each moment is the end of something, good or bad, and the beginning of something, good or bad. To the gifted, a bad ending does not give rise to a good beginning, nor does a good ending give birth to something bad.

From Matthew 25 they learn that nothing escapes the notice and judgment of Christ. All that is done, good or bad, has a one-to-one correlation in their relationship with Christ. Whatever is done *now* is either for or against Christ, the judge of all things. Current and authentic prophets cannot separate anything done for or against anyone else from Christ. Because everything, to the persons gifted with prophecy, has an absolute relationship with Christ, they are sincere, bold, dogmatic, and persistent in their pronouncements and actions.

When they make a pronouncement, they do not believe they have to quote the Bible for verification. Today's message carries the same power of biblical pronouncements; both issue from the same Holy Spirit. The Spirit, to them, is not less powerful and active today than during the biblical period. There is no time to God; God is the same today as yesterday. Goodness, righteousness, and justice are as powerful today as they were yesterday. However, today's prophets do not construe that the active presence of God's spirit now makes the Bible outdated or valueless. To the contrary, they see in the Bible similar issues, events, conditions, and persons and discover how the Spirit inspired and equipped others to respond to God's will.

For example, they perceive Armageddon as something real in biblical times and equally real in our times, though not involving the same nations, personalities, and geographic location. They see antichrist not as a distinctive person with a name, weight, height, birth date, and position but as any personification of evil, unrighteousness, and injustice, whether wrapped up in one person, twelve persons, an institution, a nation, or a philosophy. The distinguishing characteristic of antichrist is defiance of God's self-disclosure in Christ and God's offer of redemption. Divine judgment is not merely future, to them, but whenever God's will is done, denied, or rejected (see Matt. 25).

Service

The Greek word for "service" is *diakonia*. It carries a special act of servanthood possible in various ways. Its basic manifestation is in ordinary tasks that center on the worship of God. The definition is *the extraordinary ability to elevate any needed ministry or act that aids the church or another person to holy and sacred acts of worship without concern or desire for rank, popularity, or recognition.* This gift, unlike its sister gift of helps, is God-centered.

Diakonia is often translated in English as "ministry," which comes from a Latin word *minus*. This word suggests a humble and lowly state—not inferior, but gratefully humble. Humility, however, was not the original Greek understanding of the word. The Greeks, during the time of Jesus, used *diakonia* (service) to describe a social position of self-abasement or forced humiliation represented by waiting on tables, serving food and wine, or cleaning up after meals. Jesus brought a new meaning to the word by transforming such acts into honorable and loving service. He modeled service with his washing the dirty feet of the disciples (see John 13). You will find other references in Gifts' Definitions and Biblical References.

The essence of our Lord's life was his obeying and honoring God. Although his works for human beings did not necessarily benefit God, they gave testimony of God's holiness and sovereignty. The gift of service, therefore, carries the same dominant theme, honoring God through loving and caring deeds toward others. Matthew 25 is a key text to support this theme. Whatever we do for others, even the most basic and mundane things, is done unto Christ. Christ is our way to God.

Isn't this just like a loving God to make it possible for certain members of the body of Christ to have esteem and distinction, even though they are not of a priestly order? It is easy for us to look upon certain persons with priestly offices and tasks as being more important because they have high visibility and social recognition. The gift of service offsets this tendency in the body of Christ. Paul addresses himself to this spiritual ranking in 1 Corinthians 12.

Men and women with the gift of service will respond to any need without concern for social importance or rank. They respond not so much out of the apparent needs of others as their need to worship God. To them, the worship of God goes beyond sitting in a sanctuary singing, praying, listening to sermons, and offering money. Every deed of kindness is an act of worship. They can work in the kitchen, clean the floors, mow the grass, paint rooms or halls, and polish a brass cross with as much of a joyful sense of the presence of God as the teacher, pastor, healer, or administrator.

These gifted persons often display physical stamina and stick-to-itiveness beyond belief. They do not hesitate to spend personal funds to get the needed supplies for the work. The work is vital because it is an act of divine worship. They are prone to complete all tasks, and then some.

To them, when a task is incomplete, worship is incomplete, and incomplete work for God is missing the mark, a sin. They tend to be fastidious and painstakingly thorough in all that they do. They experience God in everything and believe God deserves the finest they can offer.

There are some precautions. Many persons gifted with service are likely to go overboard or do too much. They tend to get overly involved because of the delight and joy derived from serving. Also, their quick response and thoroughness in service may prompt suspicion of self-advancement and, thus, jealousy from others. These gifted persons must understand that others may not share their delight and enthusiasm for menial tasks. Their insistence on serving rather than being served may be interpreted by others as a form of rejection of others' attempts to express the same gift or the gift of helps.

The essence of the gift is not imperatives, law, or power, not position or status, not rank or authority, not dignity or esteem, but service to Christ through the church, the body of Christ. The variety within this one *charisma* is as great and numerous as the variety and number of needs within the body of Christ and what the church sees as needs in the world, which leads to the chief caution about this gift.

Emphasizing this gift's relationship to the body of Christ and its assessment of needs guards against an individualistic use of a *charisma* that is not nourished and directed by the body. Simultaneously, we need to stress and encourage the essence of grace, God's unconditional love and freedom. By this, we protect ourselves against fanaticism (*charismata* [gift] without a body) or whitewashed sepulcherism (a body [the church] without *charismata*).

Singleness

I choose to use *singleness* rather than *celibacy*. The latter is a term that does not come from the New Testament but from church tradition.

Many persons are blessed with the spiritual gift of singleness. Paul writes of singleness in 1 Corinthians 7:7, 32-35 as a *charisma*. He uses *charisma* to describe his singleness, which is an unmarried state to equip him and others to give more time and energy to the church. That does not mean all unmarried persons have this gift or no married persons have this gift.

The Greek word for "singleness" is *agamos*, which means "to be unmarried," "unbound," "unattached." The whole seventh chapter of 1 Corinthians emphasizes the presence and absence of this gift. The definition is *the extraordinary ability to offer God and the church a life unbound by marriage and free of sexual frustrations and social attachments so that one may spend the time and energy necessary for building up the church.*

No small amount of guilt has been imposed on many persons who wish to remain single. Our perception of persons who remain single usually carries a stigma resulting from bad theology and church practices that assert the ultimate purpose for life is to reproduce a like kind.

Traditional theology makes no attempt to excuse anyone from this unalterable will of God, except in the cases of illness, retardation, injury, and Roman Catholic priesthood and the nunnery. Church activities and programs are aimed mainly at serving the family and rarely consider singles. Singles have been treated as second-class citizens in God's kingdom. Therefore, many, who could have been healthier, happier, and more productive as singles who were childless, have been coerced into marriage and parenthood.

Since the 1960s, however, numerous Christian men and women have discovered a joyful ability to live a single life without the stigmatized trappings of expected sexual promiscuity in either heterosexuality or homosexuality. These persons are not antisocial and do not have a distaste for human fellowship and social intimacies. Their spirituality leads them to concentrate their interests and energies on a fuller intimacy with Christ in unhindered service to the church.

They do not lose their sensitivity toward intimate relationships. Their intimacies reveal different dimensions. They are conscious of their sexuality, but they have a special spiritual power to keep intimacies and sexual proclivities in perspective and under control. They feel an urgency to give the proper amount of attention and energies to situations that could be hampered by responsibilities in marriage and family life. They do not feel a morbid loneliness or deprivation of intimacy. Theirs is a sense of joy and liberation to be free to serve the body of Christ without hindrance.

Many who became single through death or divorce discovered they had the gift of *agamos* and chose to remain single. This does not mean that the priests, nuns, and married persons did not have that gift while in their former condition (spiritual gifts are given at spiritual rebirth). Circumstances brought to light the gift, so they now use it with great joy.

I offer a word of encouragement to persons who have problems with singleness. A young adult male came to me in secret to discuss his yearning to remain single to serve God fully, and he confessed an unquenchable sexual drive. Masturbation gave him the needed physical release but left him with severe guilt feelings. If, indeed, this man has the gift of singleness, God has also given him the power and grace not to be frustrated by sexual needs.

God doesn't play games with us. We play games with ourselves and God. God equips us with extraordinary power, the Holy Spirit (see Acts 1:8), to fulfill God's will and use of spiritual gifts (see Rom. 11:29). We are not free of suffering, but we are free from bringing suffering, such as guilt, upon ourselves. Habituation does not indicate a natural or divine condition. It is more an addiction than nature. The only way to break a habit is to stop reinforcing it. By not doing it, the mind and body will find a new level of comfort and joy. Not doing it also opens us to receive the healing grace of God. This applies to having sexual intercourse, eating wrong foods, smoking, drinking, or taking drugs.

There is another word of caution here. Suppose a person believes, feels, or finds that he or she has the gift of singleness while married. Should a divorce be sought? No! God's grace is greater than grace-gifts. And everyone has more than one gift. Circumstances may prevent us from using a certain gift, and we should be able to accept that fact without guilt. Our responsibility is not to create circumstances to accommodate the gifts but to be obedient in the use of gifts when opportunities present themselves. Let us use our other gifts fully and obediently and trust God for provisions related to the others.

We can say the same about all spiritual gifts. We cannot be loving and caring if we force the body to recognize and receive our gifts. That is the error of projection Paul tried to correct in 1 Corinthians 12–13. The gifts are to serve the body, not ourselves. If the body rejects our gifts, we are not to impose them on the body, nor are we to feel guilty over not being able to use them. We wait! God's agenda operates not to be convenient for us but to build up the body. Also, we have other gifts the body needs. So we pour our loving and caring obedience into them.

A widow described to me her battle with guilt after learning she had the gift of singleness. Many friends and family members thought she ought to remarry, but she was not inclined—and she wondered why. Her marriage had been a happy and fulfilling one. She could think of no reason why it couldn't be repeated, but she didn't want to remarry. Eventually, she discovered she had the gift of singleness, and she had greater guilt for a while. She said, "I loved my husband. We had a good marriage. Yet, being single is greater. I love being without a mate. I feel so liberated. Is there something wrong with me?" It was a comfort to her to learn that Paul went through similar struggles (see 2 Cor. 12:7-9) and came to the conclusion that God's grace is sufficient.

Care must be taken not to settle on something's being a spiritual gift until we devote enough time and experience for confirmation. Our understanding of God is never complete, and the heart of faith is always a mystery. But God eventually confirms our gifts. We often get into situations, such as marriage and childbearing, without knowing God had other plans for us. Our loving God provides healing grace through forgiveness. The opportunity to fulfill our divine destiny will come. That is for sure. However, let us not mistake real guilt over a real situation for a spiritual gift.

For example, some people never live up to their marriage and parental vows because of neglect or distractions. Once death occurs or some other kind of separation, they experience emotional liberation, which could very well be an escape mechanism to rid themselves of real guilt. It is unfair to credit this feeling to the discovery of a spiritual gift until the past has been dealt with. To imagine that pleasant feelings over ignoring the past is a *charisma* is to invite some hard and painful moments that will surely come. The past needs to be worked through with honesty, much prayer, and counseling.

Yet, a long-suppressed or denied *charisma* of singleness may surface because of appropriate circumstances (death or divorce). If this is the case, look for confirmations of the gift from God. As we practice any gift, our faith matures and drives illicit feelings into oblivion. The practice of a gift, furthermore, should be aimed not at feelings or emotions of any kind but at loyalty to Christ in a shared ministry. Then and only then can the gift effectively build up the body of Christ.

Spirit-Music

After experiencing a spiritual awakening— often called baptism of the Holy Spirit—many people suddenly acquire musical abilities. To distinguish this gift from musical abilities acquired through interests, skills, and training, I call this spirit-music. Their newfound freedom in Christ reveals a gift of which they were not aware. Some of them had very little, if any, prior interest or aptitude for music. Now they write lyrics or musical scores, or both; some begin to sing; others take up musical instruments through which they praise God and inspire the body of Christ, the church.

Several of these persons have demonstrated their musical gift for me. One woman came to my church study and asked if I would be willing to listen to her sing in the sanctuary. She said she had never sung before but discovered that God wanted her to sing. An associate and I accompanied her to the sanctuary where she prayed at the altar and then sang for us. It was an electrifying experience for us. We did not recognize the language of her music, so we asked if she could sing it in English. She said, "I'll find out." She knelt again at the communion rail and after a moment rose and sang in English. Her voice, lyrics, and score were a rare spiritual treat.

In another church, two women shared with me their gifts of music. One played the guitar while singing music she had written; the other played the piano and wrote the music for what she played. Neither had ever done this before, and both were inspiring others with their spirit-music.

I shared these stories with a group in another church. After the workshop, someone suggested that a participant demonstrate her gift of spirit-music. The woman lovingly and enthusiastically went to the piano to play. She asked me if I had a preference of a song for her to play. I learned that she could play any piece of music that she had ever heard, although she had never had a lesson. Her playing was profoundly skillful and moving. She had been given this gift of music to bless the church.

These cases represent just some of the rare ones I know about. Others tell me of many more persons who are thus blessed. But acquired and cultivated musical abilities are also included as spirit-music. A young woman who plays the Autoharp and sings has developed her natural abilities and dedicated them to God. When she plays and sings, I see an aura of spiritual power that surrounds her. I am moved to blissful tears as she spiritualizes her music. The Holy Spirit transforms her acquired and trained skills into channels for spiritual blessings. I am a grateful and blessed recipient of God's grace through her.

I've listened to another young woman dozens of times. Congregations melt into spiritual bliss when she sings. I have been equally moved by the way she engages her mind, soul, and body in her singing. She shared with me that she doesn't sing unless she knows the time and music are right. When she attempted to sing merely because she was asked or wanted to, it did not feel right, and others were not edified. She told me how she could alter her seriously sick daughter's blood pressure and slow down her racing heart by singing to her. As she sang, the monitors hooked up to her daughter told the story. I believe monitors hooked up to her congregational auditors would tell the same story!

We ought to be able to mark the difference between performance music and spiritual music. Let me emphasize, however, that performance is fine within its limited scope. Entertainment and spirituality are not mutually exclusive. It's all right to have fun and to enjoy quality activities. God filled the universe with attributes to fill the five senses with awe and wonder. We ought to fill our ministries with performances to match the natural needs of our senses. Nevertheless, a deeper part of humanity, our spiritual nature, is larger than the five senses. Since the senses may be the main routes to the spirit, we must make sure that the vehicles carry the appropriate cargo. The gift of spirit-music serves these needs.

Spirit-music is the *extraordinary ability to receive and to share musical lyrics and tunes as messages from God to help others to experience Christian love, to inspire them to Christian service, and to win others to Christ.* Specific references to this gift are 1 Corinthians 14:15 and Ephesians 5:19. Others appear in Gifts' Definitions and Biblical References.

These gifted persons believe in and experience the presence of the Holy Spirit. Many of them hear the music, as Mozart claimed he did. They have a strong urge and urgency to obey musical inclinations, whether to create or perform, immediately, or they lose the power of the moment. Many of them do not use their music gift until they receive a confirmation either from scripture or from a prompting of the Holy Spirit. Most of their lyrics are steeped in biblical language, and they believe their music is a message from God directed to someone or some group for spiritual reasons.

God does not exclude persons who do not write original music. These persons have a spiritual sensitivity that tells them when they are under the inspiration of God's spirit. They are inclined to pray for God's guidance in selecting the right music for certain occasions. They do not consider their act a performance. Here we encounter a variety of motivations for spiritual music.

Some consider their musical activity a form of worship. Usually, these persons have the accompanying gift of service (see "Service" entry). Others perceive their mission in music as inspirational and encouraging; they often have the gift of exhortation. Education or information about the good news of Christ is the focus of many singers. They have the gift of evangelism or teaching. I mention only one more possibility: the spiritual musician with the gift of helps. Many musicians, instrumentalists and singers, do not enjoy doing solos. Their mission is to help others, and what a mission! Their spirit-music is a support ministry. Without them, the body is incomplete—musically and emotionally lifeless.

To determine how your music fits into the church's ministry, meditate on your music and whatever gives you the greatest enjoyment. Take that to the descriptions of all gifts in this book and ponder their various behavior characteristics. You may discover that your music is, indeed, a gift of spirit-music to build up the body of Christ.

12

No Lack of Gifts

Paul assured the Corinthians that they lacked no spiritual gifts (see 1 Cor. 1:7). That biblical word applies to us today. The church's opportunities for serving its members and the world are covered by these extraordinary abilities we recognize as gifts. Let's look at more of them!

Suffering

We face a mystery here, if not a paradox. People who seek or pray for certain gifts usually go after self-serving ones. They want high visibility, social esteem, and something emotionally enjoyable. I have not met anyone who sought the gift of suffering or, for that matter, consciously wants to suffer. Yet, God, the loving Redeemer and Healer, the One upon whom most call for comfort and ease, gives certain persons hardships, pain, and discomforts as a means to minister to others! The best New Testament examples are Paul and Jesus.

Paul speaks often about his suffering and suggests to Timothy that his rekindled gift may also bring Timothy suffering (see 2 Cor. 11:23-27; 12:7-10; 2 Tim. 1:6-10). Although suffering is not specifically identified by the word *charisma* in scripture, it is implicit enough and too evident as a means of divinely purposeful ministry to pass over without serious consideration.

The definition of suffering is *the extraordinary ability to endure hardship, pain, and distress with such an amount of joy and strength to inspire others to endure their suffering and to lead others to accept*

God's loving redemption made possible in Christ's suffering. It comes from a Greek word *paschein*, meaning "to suffer because of beliefs and the practice of beliefs." It means "to be punished, abused, threatened, insulted, discriminated against, or victimized by injustice because of the Christian faith." This gift is not the same as martyrdom, which is a powerful witness. "To suffer" or *paschein* is actually identifying with and taking on the real affliction of Christ. It is a validation of being a chosen vessel for specific ministries (see 2 Cor. 11:23ff.).

The most effective means of God's self-disclosure was the suffering and death of Jesus Christ. We celebrate these events in Holy Communion, Mass, the Lord's Supper, or the Eucharist—whatever we wish to call it. We celebrate our Lord's suffering and death at each person's baptism. One understanding of baptism is to be "buried" with Christ (see Col. 2:12). Our Lord's preparation for death and his dying were no easy moments. The cross was ignominious. Nothing could have been more disgraceful, inglorious, base, and vile than for such a loving and selfless person to be so treated. Yet, Jesus bore his cross (suffering) with faithfulness and perseverance.

He also revealed that others must bear their cross if they are to be his disciples (see Matt. 10:38; Mark 8:34). So, to a great extent, every Christian is given the role of suffering (see Rom. 5:3; Phil. 1:27-29). Furthermore, God gives to others the gift of carrying the affliction of Christ as a special means to serve the kingdom. This cross bearing may not be martyrdom (something we have come to know as dying for Christ), but it is an inner struggle with anxiety and conflict. It could be a life-style and social standing one's faithful witness imposes. Luke apparently added "daily" to taking up the cross to suggest suffering emotionally, socially, or mentally rather than physically (see 9:23).

Another point about life-style suffering for faith in Christ applies to persons and their position in admired and glamorized situations. Many successful businesspersons suffer greatly because of their sense of mission to give witness to the power of integrity and honesty in the business world. The successful businesspersons I know work longer and harder hours than their employees. This tendency is particularly true of authentic Christian businesspersons. Theirs is a severe type of suffering for Christ.

I know professional, executive, and business women who feel called to their newly assumed freedoms and privileges, but who suffer deeply to retain their positions as a means of witnessing as Christians. I know pastors and denominational leaders who suffer greatly because of their mission to bring honesty and integrity to hierarchical positions or large churches. While others admire and envy them, they admire and almost envy others with fewer responsibilities. Gifted leaders and administrators may prefer a simpler life-style but feel they must remain in these positions because of their faith, and they sometimes suffer for it. The point is that not only the poor, the unemployed, and the unhealthy suffer. The gifted just may be included in the poor in spirit.

We make a serious mistake to assign all suffering to the power of Satan, as some persons do. A survey of scripture shows that suffering is bad, yet it is also of God and is assigned by God for divine purposes. The following biblical principles concern positive values of suffering.

1. *Suffering is not always caused by sin or the absence of faith* (see 1 Cor. 4:9-14; 2 Cor. 11:22-31).

2. *Suffering is often used to make us aware of God's power to sustain us* (see Psalm 68:19; 2 Cor. 12:9-10). Satan would never aid us in this way!

3. *Suffering often causes people, good and evil, to praise God* (see John 9:1-3; 11:4; 1 Pet. 1:6-7; Rev. 11:13). Satan would have us to curse God.

4. *Suffering teaches us humility* (see 2 Cor. 12:7). Can we imagine Satan teaching such a thing?

5. *Suffering is used to perfect and strengthen us for righteousness* (see Psalm 66:8-9; Heb. 2:10; 12:10).

6. *Suffering creates fellowship and community and motivates us to use our gifts for the common good* (see Phil. 4:12-15; 1 Pet. 4:12).

7. *Suffering leads to hope that only grace provides* (see 1 Pet. 1:6, 13).

8. *Suffering is no cause for shame* (see 2 Tim. 1:12).

9. *Suffering helps us to understand and appreciate further knowledge of Christ* (see Phil. 3:8).

10. *Suffering teaches us to be frail* (see Psalm 14:6), *to give thanks* (see 2 Cor. 1:11), *to increase our faith* (see Psalm 46:10), and *to comfort and strengthen others who suffer and are weak* (see 2 Cor. 1:3-11; Phil. 1:12-14, 20; 2:17; Heb. 2:18).

This list is a mere token of the rich teachings in scripture about the positive value of suffering. It is also true that Satan uses suffering in an attempt to discredit God, Christ, and Christians. Satan wants us to think that suffering is never the will of God, and that healing *now* is God's full and immediate will. Unfortunately, this appeal is to a hedonistic trait in human nature, which is the desire for pleasure and the avoidance of pain. Satan inspires this approach in many ministries, especially on television and healing campaigns. The fact is, we will never get out of this life alive, and usually some type of suffering accompanies dying and death—if not for the dying, certainly for their loved ones. We would be better served by using our energy and time looking realistically at the positive dimensions of suffering noted in scripture rather than avoidance and Satan's use of that.

There is much evidence for a spiritual gift of suffering, in and beyond the Bible. The most prominent characteristic of persons who may have this gift is the lack of complaining. Someone said, "Health is more than the lack of sickness." Something similar can be said of suffering—it is more than the presence of complaints or visible symptoms. Just because persons do not complain of physical or emotional pain does not mean they do not suffer. The spiritual gift often prohibits verbalizing the suffering, except when it offers an opportunity to give a positive witness to faith. An illustration is fasting, a religious act that certainly brings discomfort. Jesus rebuked persons who made public displays of their fasting pains by looking dismal and disfiguring their faces (see Matt. 6:16-17). I am sure he would disapprove of any self-serving displays of one's gift of suffering.

Persons with the gift of suffering know deeply that God is working a divine plan through it. They have an intuition of providence and hope. Persons with suffering do not easily blame circumstances or others for discomforts. They often perceive others and circumstances as God's avenues for grace-sufferings. They never project suffering on others as a means of God's grace for them. In fact, persons with the gift of suffering absorb the pain and distress of others. They are spiritual sponges to receive and to soak up the painful energy of others. You never hear them speak of the devil as the manager of their lives and condition. Rather, they feel called of God.

They readily identify with others who hurt. When others describe or complain about their suffering, the gifted do not engage in a one-up match with them. They rarely speak of their own pain, and then only when it lets the other sufferers know that they are not alone (see 2 Cor. 1:3-7). The gifted sufferers do not petition prayer groups and congregations to pray for their healing but may gracefully ask for prayers for strength and perseverance. They may even offer prayers of thanksgiving for their suffering (see Phil. 4:6).

Gifted sufferers do not die from their suffering. Paul did not die from his thorn, unless it was his faith and stubborn refusal to give up Christ. Jesus did not die from his suffering. Even his death was a cup the Father gave him (see Matt. 26:39; Mark 14:36; Luke 22:42; John 18:11). For Christ, suffering was a part of his entire life; if anything, death delivered him from it. So it is with those he chooses to suffer as he suffered.

Gifted sufferers have an extraordinary amount of joy. Joy is not an emotion or a feeling, but it has emotional expressions. Joy is not the same as happiness. Happiness is a feeling or an emotion, sometimes experienced even in the midst of suffering. Joy is the most basic component of the Greek word for "gift," *charisma*. The *char* stem supplies other prominent words in faith talk: "rejoicing" (*chario*), "thanksgiving" (*eucharisteo*), "grace" (*charis*), and "blessing" or "bestowing" (*charizomai*). Joy is an inner strength that transforms pain and hardships into clear visions of hope and fulfillment. This hope transports the gifted sufferer beyond the immediate sources of pain into the presence of eternal peace, even God (see Phil. 4:7).

Teaching

Ideally, the gifts should be arranged according to similarities. But an alphabetical sequence is a quicker aid to find any gift for study. We've just switched from a very heavy-duty gift to one that is less mysterious and controversial. However, the gift of teaching serves all the gifts in its power to explain, elucidate, and apply to daily Christian living. Maybe its position in the sequence isn't faulty after all.

"Teaching" comes from the Greek *didaskalia*, which means "to teach," "to instruct," "to clarify," "to elucidate," "to illuminate," "to simplify," and "to illustrate for the sake of communication and understanding." Specific references to this spiritual gift are 1 Corinthians

12:28 and Ephesians 4:11. Other are listed in Gifts' Definitions and Biblical References.

As a spiritual gift (*charisma*), teaching is a ministry of instructing and clarifying things about God and our response to God under the influence of the Holy Spirit. The definition is *the extraordinary ability to discern, analyze, and deliver biblical and other spiritual truths to help others to comprehend and accept the clear calling of God to live justly and righteously.*

Communication is the key to the power of this gift. Communication is a two-way flow of energy. Communication is not complete without an appropriate response. An appropriate response does not have to be agreement, but it does require understanding. The person gifted with teaching has the ability to communicate to the degree that the hearers or readers will understand what is being taught.

The essential subject matter of the spiritual gift is the presence of the living Christ as Lord and Savior. Spiritual teaching is more than objective data, more than mere biblical material; it is a communication of a subjective experience with the risen Lord. Anyone can read, memorize, and recite biblical verses. We read in the Bible that the devil knows enough to quote scripture (see Luke 4:10). Spiritual teaching, however, practices no laziness toward careful and thorough studying to demonstrate divine approval and effectiveness (see 2 Tim. 2:15).

We make a serious error in the field of Christian education, and I believe it is catching up with us. We follow a secular model for teaching the faith. In fact, we think that if a person is a professional teacher in secular institutions, she or he ought to teach in the body of Christ, the church. Many urban and rural churches boast of their number of teachers with college or university degrees. I served several of these, especially one on a university campus. Some persons who wanted to attend church school said that they were told, "If you don't have a college degree, you'd better not go to that church's classes." God doesn't operate that way. When we see how Jesus chose his disciples, we must recognize that we have departed from a pattern of giftedness and selection made by God.

Somehow we must recognize that few things are diminishing in our churches more rapidly and dramatically than education. Apparently, the higher we raise the standards for Christian education, that is, based on written materials and qualifications for teachers, the faster the decline.

Yet, nearly every denomination declares education is the key to sincere discipleship and church growth, citing Matthew 28:19-20.

More money is put into education than most other ministries combined. The proofs are the educational building, its maintenance, and the professional educator of many churches, not to mention the amount spent on literature. Yet, nearly every church is stunned by its decline in enrollment and attendance. We have to conclude that the amount of money, dedicated building space, trained leaders, and spiffy materials are failing us. Is there a solution?

I believe the solution is a return to the charismatic teaching found in the Bible. This teaching depends on an experience of and direction from the Holy Spirit. There is no other way to describe the fast growth and spread of Christianity during its formative years. Let's face it. They didn't have seminaries and Christian colleges to crank out preachers and directors of education. They had only the raw material of a holy alliance with God.

To be fair, however, we must point out that Paul was highly educated, and Jesus obviously knew the language and customs of his Jewish heritage and probably much of the gentile world around him. For the most part, early Christians were illiterate; yet, they were so far advanced in their understanding of God and God's will for life, our finest schools and theologians today blush with embarrassment over how far behind we remain.

A key to this mystery may be found in a survey of the early church's treatment of the Holy Spirit. It was extremely vital with conversions and dynamic growth at first, but it began to slow down by the same degree by which it declined in its references to the Holy Spirit. Its literary references to the Holy Spirit decreased as the church increased its dependence on formal education, especially the secular model. The Pastoral Epistles reveal this trend. The later these are dated, the fewer references they make to the Holy Spirit. This trend is easily traced throughout our history. Exceptions are found, though, when certain dramatic and radical events took place: the Reformation, the Protestant movement, the Wesleyan revival, the Pentecostal movement, and charismatic renewal. If it is a fact that we write about things that interest, stir, and move us, this may show us our way back.

With few exceptions, we still use the secular model of education to empower us with understanding. In most attempts to supply those rooms in our educational building and to assure us of attendance, which is now questionable, we rarely seek only born again Christians (see John 3:3), persons who give witness to their being "in Christ" (2 Cor. 5:17) or "transformed" (Rom. 12:2), to say nothing of persons who have been "filled with the Spirit" (Eph. 5:18). I have approached this subject in several churches and was told that this way of doing things is getting too personal. Others said that they would not dare do such a thing—their classes would have no teachers at all! So what do we want, a living body of Christ or a corpse of an institution?

Charismatic teaching is different from secular methods. While charismatic teachers place importance on research, accuracy of details, and correct meanings, they also radiate with an enthusiastic devotion to Christ as a personal Lord that permeates all they do. They delight in reading the Bible for personal devotions as well as the primary source of teaching material and discover the Bible is full of relevant messages for today. Charismatic teachers are more inclined to search out the meaning of scripture than to memorize verses, events, names, and titles of books. Yet, they consider these additional aids to personal spiritual development.

Teaching (*didaskalia*) becomes more than transmitting information; it carries a deeply relational feature that causes teachers to identify with their students on a personal level, one that engages their own emotions to identify with the hurts, pains, aspirations, and hopes of the students. This gifted teaching is more than methodology, technique, or subject matter. It is a reciprocal companionship that helps teacher and student as they move together toward perfection in Christ. This kind of Christian teacher finds no satisfaction in simply delivering a lesson if there is no personal relationship outside. This charismatic quality of teaching insists on a partnership with the learners. The student teaches as much as is learned, and the teacher learns as much as is taught.

That many astute and articulate scholars have places in classrooms of higher education does not mean they have the spiritual gift of teaching. Their offering is of unquestionable value, but it is a mistake to assume that they have the *charisma*. The difference is extraordinary. Persons who have been to seminary, a college where Christian professors teach, to a church school classroom, or to worship services where they heard people with this gift know the difference. Even books written by authors who have the gift read differently.

The charismatic teacher displays three inseparable attributes of familiarity, whether in public or in print. First, this teacher demonstrates an unquestionable familiarity with God. Divine presence saturates the teacher's personality and shows up in everything he or she does. Second, the teacher has a unique relationship to the subject matter. The Bible or other sacred subject being taught is more than impersonal data. It is like a dear friend the teacher fondly introduces to the students (or readers). Third, a bond that connects the teacher and the students to one another transcends the traditional teaching-learning process. The bond is a spiritual partnership, each giving to the other a way to experience God.

Persons with this gift delight in researching meticulous details. They are never lazy in preparations. They do not let any of these three familiarities suffice for the neglect of the others. They tend to verbalize their feelings about teaching materials and purpose for teaching. They are keenly interested in validating new information by acceptable and proved methods of verification. They will not accept propositional truths, scriptural accuracies or inaccuracies, doctrinal exactitude, and theological dogmas without tested methods of weighing their value for today's living. John Wesley's carefully designed method of validation ("Quadrilateral of Authority") is an example: the appeal to Scripture, Tradition, Experience, and Reason. The heart of the spiritual gift of teaching is discipling (see Matt. 28:19).

Teaching is not done just in a classroom of students. It is also done through music, paintings, drama, and various types of writings. Although a face-to-face setting for teaching is probably the most effective, the others are just as legitimate as *charismata*. Consider the New Testament's impact on us today. No question about it, it is a living word no less powerful today than it was initially. The writers, whoever they were, inform and inspire more people today than ever before. Others—scholars, writers, poets, musicians, and painters—carry the same energizing power of the Holy Spirit.

The grace of God transcends all limitations of time, distance, and means. This active grace, transported by God's spirit, brings to the present moment the dynamic reality of the three familiarities, namely, God, the material (message), and the audience. Whenever we open ourselves to these sources of God's grace, we know that we are in touch with extraordinary persons through extraordinary means.

Voluntary Poverty

Although this gift may have a strong sting of disapproval, there is too much evidence in church history and among many later Christians to dismiss the possibility of its being a spiritual gift. At least, Paul implies that it is a spiritual gift in the first part of 1 Corinthians 13:3. It is also demonstrated in the lives of many persons and institutions throughout history. It is an *extraordinary ability to live a simple, conservative, and unencumbered life free of material responsibilities in order to devote large amounts of time, energy, and other resources to essential ministries.* Some scholars of *charismata* call this gift voluntary poverty. However, we see this gift in the same light we consider all other gifts. We do not have a choice in the gifts we receive from God, but we *do choose* (volunteer, if you will) to use them. In this light, all gifts are voluntarily operated.

Our Lord, the divine Son of God, possessed all the gifts. Perhaps others are more illustrative of ordinary examples of this extraordinary ability. I disagree with the tendency to think that the gift of poverty is the flip side of the gift of giving. My observations lead me to believe the gift of giving is replenished with a special power to increase one's supply in order to give more. One cannot give what one does not have.

The gift of poverty is to live in freedom from responsibilities that possessions require. In poverty one gives time, energy, influence, and skills—not money. Yet, when persons with the gift of poverty receive amounts of money beyond their simple needs, they give money. One thinks of Paul, Francis of Assisi, John Wesley, and Mother Teresa. Poverty to them was not a circumstantial or providential hindrance from owning and enjoying more of worldly goods. If anything, they worked hard at maintaining a lower than normal level of material ownership. St. Francis gave away his belongings. John Wesley maintained a standard of living that cost him only thirty pounds per year but gave away thirty thousand pounds during the course of his life. The only boast he could make of material goods was of two silver spoons, one in London and the other in Bristol—probably gifts with great symbolism.

This characteristic determines the essential difference between being poor and practicing the gift of poverty. Universally, poor people, those caught in circumstances beyond their control, spend their energies trying to survive or to emerge from their sad plight. Persons with the gift of poverty move in the opposite direction. They strive rigorously not to have material things for one of two reasons: poverty helps them to identify with the poor they wish to serve, or they seek to be free from the demands of material possessions to give themselves more fully to others. The others in this latter sense may be poor or well-off. This facet of the gift of poverty perceives others as needing more than material goods. So they spend their skills, time, and energies to serve the needs of others.

Certain aspects of the gift of poverty apply to all members of the body of Christ. Everyone needs to be seriously sensitive to disparities of ownerships and levels of opportunities to serve one another's needs. This application can be taken too far or not far enough. The primitive church tried and failed to impose this poverty on all members of the church (see Acts 2:45); thus, it went too far. An example of not going far enough is the young man who sought perfection but refused to exercise his gift of poverty (see Mark 10:17-22).

One prominent feature of persons with the gift of poverty is that they do not think of themselves as poor, although they may live on less money than most poor people around them. They do not feel that this economic status is an imposition. They have a sense of freedom poor people and rich people alike do not have. They are very industrious as they spend extraordinary amounts of energy improving the lives and conditions of others, all others—not just the poor. Because many spend much of their time raising funds, but neither for themselves nor their "kind," they are heroically successful among the rich and the poor. Many choose not to marry or to have children to avoid interfering with their calling to give themselves to others without hindrances.

There are faithful Christians with this gift in marriage, family life, and even business. That is not a contradiction. While there are varieties of gifts (see 1 Cor. 12:4), there are also varieties (levels?) of ways of ministering (see 12:5). I know Christian couples and families who could be much better off financially if they did not choose to give generously to others. Theirs is not the gift of giving but the gift of living an extraordinarily simple life so that others may reap the fruit of their spiritual gift.

Their simple and conservative life does not provide money and more money to give to others; rather, they devote more time and energy to serve others in many other ways, which may include money.

The gift of giving is more typical of the widow and her oil and flour (see 1 Kings 17). The more one gives, the more God provides for one to give. The gift of poverty is more typical of Elijah in the same story. Both sought to obey the voice of God for their lives. The key to this gift is not how much or how little one must have to please God, or how much or how little one must give to others. It is an unencumbered life-style of simplicity that frees one to serve faithfully and fully God's choice of needs (see Mark 10:21). Often, though the simplified life-style is not designed by the recipient of this gift, when God maneuvers circumstances to establish it, he or she accepts it with joy and serenity.

Wisdom

"Wisdom" comes from *sophia* in Greek and means "a practical application of knowledge (divine or natural) to specific and concrete situations that call on God's favor (grace)." The main reference to this gift is 1 Corinthians 12:8; others appear in Gifts' Definitions and Biblical References.

The definition of the gift is *the extraordinary ability to make concrete and specific applications of divine knowledge received directly from God, from one's spiritual gift of knowledge, or from another's shared gift or gifts.* I think it is an error to consider this gift a flash of divine insight or imagination expressed in a word or an utterance. I find persons with this gift to be stable and consistent in wise (applicable) behavior and words. They show a wide range of intelligence about many subjects and ministries. This intelligence is not stored data to impress but practical methods and procedures for negotiating a wide range of ministries, if not problems.

These gifted persons are able to act, speak, write, or draw to apply God's eternal and lofty truths to the concrete realities of daily living and ministering to others. They often appear to have an uncanny ability to make statements that, at first, do not make sense but eventually solve serious problems simply and thoroughly. An example is Augustine's oft-repeated phrase, "Love and do what you will." Its simplicity is sometimes embarrassing. To be sure, when we truly love God, we will do whatever God wants; and that will please not only God but also us. The wisdom of this statement captures all that Paul writes in the Book of Romans about law and grace.

Many times, the spiritually wise do not realize the wisdom of their statements or actions, but they feel compelled to express themselves, despite possible challenges or charges of being simpleminded. What they say often brings to light the hidden but obvious truth. It simply rings true.

Charismatically wise persons cut through much folderol and ask practical questions or offer sensible suggestions that embarrass the rest of us with their sting of realism. For example, when an adulteress was in danger of being stoned to death, Jesus stooped and wrote something in the sand as her accusers looked on. We do not know what he wrote, but it was enough to cause her accusers to leave in a peaceful hurry—without throwing the first stone (see John 8:3-11). Another example of spiritual wisdom applied to a concrete situation is Paul's advice to sailors during a severe storm (see Acts 27).

This gift of wisdom is also the ability to see divine and spiritual significance in seemingly insignificant or inconsequential events and situations. Persons with this gift perceive God's glory in mundane and ordinary things and people. Simply put, their heads are not so high in the clouds of theological mysteries that they cannot see God in the simple things in life.

To them, if God is not significantly present in a marriage, lovemaking, childrearing, home life, business deals, fun things, and all the problems, challenges, and joys of life, God isn't in heaven either! God is everywhere or nowhere. Spiritually wise persons do not consider God a religious being who shows up only when people pray and gather in a building called church. They experience God as a participant in the rough-and-tumble of life, bringing love, joy, peace, fun, happiness, repair, redemption, and hope. They see God in the stars, moon, planets, flowers, trees, rivers, oceans, mountains, and in hospitals, nurseries, kindergartens, battlefields, businesses, courts, and legislatures. Oh, yes, they see God in church, too!

13

Discovering Our Gifts

We have learned much about the gifts. Now let us consider methods of discovering which ones are ours. The New Testament says plenty about *charismata,* but it doesn't offer any helps for discovering them. Paul goes to great lengths to clear up some serious misunderstandings and abuses; yet, he says nothing about how to identify the gifts each person has (see 1 Cor. 12–14). If we knew for sure which gifts are ours, abuses and misuses could be reduced or eliminated. This chapter takes up one method for discovery. The Grace-Gifts Discovery Inventory amplifies another.

O.B.E.D.I.E.N.C.E.

Sometimes explicit and at other times implicit, the word *obey* or *obedience* pops up in connection with the use of spiritual gifts (see Rom. 11:29-33; *obedience* and *disobedience* are used there four times). In Romans 12:6 Paul asserts, "Having gifts that differ, . . . *let us use them"* (emphasis mine). That sounds imperative! So does 1 Peter 4:10: "As each has received a gift, *employ it* for one another" (emphasis mine). My logic says that if the "gifts and the call of God are irrevocable" as Paul states in Romans 11:29, there is this strong matter of obedience, but a joyful one. How does one obey something not known? The acrostic, O.B.E.D.I.E.N.C.E., may help us as a guide to discovery.

O = Obey the calling. The "call" in Romans 11:29 concerns being solicited, identified, and designated for something, which personalizes the giftedness. "Irrevocable" describes something that is not capable of change, no turning back. And "gift" is the blessing of God designed specifically for a ministry. Put all this together and you can make a strong case for obedience as an essential and appropriate response. Obedience is a nonnegotiable component of our fellowship and service in the body of Christ.

B = Begin a study. A call to ministry is also a call to prepare, and everyone is called. We cannot be effective ministers in the body of Christ if we do not know what we are supposed to do. So we study. Paul introduces us to the largest biblical passage that deals with gifts by saying, "Now concerning spiritual gifts, brethren, I do not want you to be uninformed" (1 Cor. 12:1). Then he engages his gift of teaching to prepare for an understanding of gifts but not how to discover who has what. Let's look at some ways to study for discovery.

One is to read what the Bible says about *charismata*. To aid your study, I have listed biblical references to the gifts in the Gifts' Definitions and Biblical References. Many church school classes use these references as their literature for several weeks; some take months. They bring their Bibles to class and let the scripture speak for itself, a method that is growing in popularity. Someone reads the definition of a gift and makes sure that everyone is focused on that gift and its definition. Another person reads a passage while the others follow in silence. A brief moment of silent meditation and reflection follows. Then they share what surfaces in their thoughts relating to the gift and the biblical reference. This sequence continues with different readers until all references have been read.

In addition, after the biblical references have been given proper attention, someone describes the characteristics peculiar to the gift under study. (Several preceding chapters of this book cover these mannerisms.) During the course of discussion, everyone is asked to think of others who may have the gift under study. If there is strong agreement over persons they think may have the gift and if they are not present, someone is delegated to speak with them and tell what has transpired. In many cases, they become interested enough to join in the study.

Another way to study the gifts is to read some of the books listed in the Bibliography at the back of this book. Since the early seventies, many books have been published that are worthy of study.

A third method of study is to observe others who obviously have certain gifts. Being a gifts watcher is made easier by studying the behavioral traits covered in the preceding chapters of this book. By becoming acquainted with some of the prominent signs in others' behavior, we can engage them in conversation about how they feel and what they believe.

E = Examine feelings and fantasies. Physiological and neurological studies reveal that religious feelings and behavior come from the right brain. This hemisphere of the brain is important to the discovery of our gifts. It is where we experience the powers of imagination and feelings. Some ways to use this creative section of the brain to discover gifts are as follows.

Fantasize having a gift. Imagine yourself with the traits explained in the section covering that gift. Picture in your mind a scenario for this gift's use and how you would use it. Project your thoughts to the results you would expect or want. Now, examine your feelings. Are they good or bad? Are you excited or fearful? This exercise requires mental energy and time but is well worth the effort. However, you must disengage the reasoning of the left brain, which will warn of lack of training, abilities, experience, and so on. You have to *imagine* having these to engage the power to feel.

God wonderfully made us (see Psalm 139:13-14). One of the valuable attributes of the human psyche is the capacity to feel. That is where we live most of the time. We make the majority of our decisions on the basis of how we feel and not what we know. To test this, I often ask, "What is the most critical decision you will make in life, except to follow Christ?" The answer is always, "Whom to marry." Then I ask, "Did you choose your spouse on the basis of information, data, or logic?" Lots of laughs ring out in reply. Everyone knows how feelings took over and rightly so. Otherwise, most of us wouldn't be here. The first force that causes an attraction toward the opposite sex is feelings—not logic or reasoning.

It's OK to test feelings. If anything doesn't feel right, it ought to be questioned. Also, we must consider the strongest component of the word *charisma*. Its foundation is "joy," the *char* word. Joy is more than feeling but cannot be separated from it. So, while experimenting with or actually practicing a gift for real, feelings should be considered. Of course, difficulties don't vanish with a gift that feels right or good. Difficulties and good or positive feelings are not mutually exclusive. With the right attitude toward discovering God's gifts, even in the midst of hardship and pain, feelings can point the way.

Dreams and fantasies are significant, too. Dreams and visions have value in the Bible. We've almost done away with dreams in our conditioning to dwell in the logic, data, and reasoning section of the brain. One way of retraining and restoring the power of the right brain is using dreams, visions, and fantasies in a wholesome manner. We need to discover God's will, and since we do not have a specific how-to section in the Bible for discovering our gifts, visioning and imagining are indispensable helps. God rewards any effort to discover our call and gifts with certainty.

D = Disciplined belief. It is one thing to believe something and another to act on the belief. Too many of us say that we believe in the Bible, but we do not take it seriously. I am addressing here persons who want to take the Bible seriously. In this connection, then, consider Romans 11:29: "For the gifts and the call of God are irrevocable." Also, reread 1 Peter 4:10: "As each has received a gift. . . ." Do you believe what you've read? Then act on it!

I have heard many people state that they must have been left out because they obviously don't have any gifts, and they profess to be Christians. They're really saying that they don't want to be responsible as Christians. If we follow Paul's use of the body imagery, no part of the human body is irresponsible. Every part was wonderfully designed to serve the body. So it is with the body of Christ, the church. No one is without gifts for ministry. But it takes faith and disciplined effort to discover and use them. Thus, *disciplined belief.*

I = Investigate the gifts of others. The study of the Bible and other sacred literature is surpassed only by closely observing people. Paul practiced and preached this principle. He instructed Timothy to remember the faith of his grandmother Lois and his mother Eunice, which Paul was sure dwelt in him (see 2 Tim. 1:5). Paul was talking about more than the general faith of all Christians; he was referring to the power of a specific faith, a spiritual gift. Also, Paul continually called attention to his gifts, though he didn't name them. Obviously, Paul believed modeling one's faith and ministry is important to others' discovering theirs.

I enjoy gifts watching. I delight in spotting traits of gifts in persons who do not know that they have a gift. It is a joy to share with them what I see happening in their ministry behavior. Once they agree that I have sized them up correctly, my understanding of the gifts is sharpened. They learn and I learn, also.

E = Experiment with the gifts. Yearning for a particular gift is OK but doesn't guarantee its acquisition. Yet, the only way to know for sure is to experiment with it. If a person does not know which gifts he or she has, it is all right to pray for a gift and experiment.

How do you know whether you have the gift of healing unless you lay hands on someone and pray for healing? How will you know if God has gifted you to receive healings unless you're willing for another to lay hands on you and pray for you? How do you know you don't have the gift of teaching unless you teach? How do you know you don't have the gift of tongues unless you try it? How do you know you don't have the gift of administration unless you agree to take a chair of responsibility that calls for that gift? How do you know you don't have the gift of evangelism unless you are willing to confront nonChristians with an invitation to follow Christ? Experimentation is important.

The Grace-Gifts Discovery Inventory will help you bring to surface some attributes of gifts you may have. I have found that most people's gifts appear in the top six of their highest scores. From there it is expedient to begin experimenting from the top down. If your top six scores are identical or two or more are the same, choose your own order to experiment. This method reduces the need to experiment with all thirty-two gifts covered.

N = Never doubt God's promises. This statement is the next-door neighbor, if not a sibling, of disciplined belief already discussed, but there's a difference. The way to overcome doubt, with which Satan plagues us, is simply to stop it. Many of us stay in a "but rut." We quote a promise of God, then allow this demon of doubt to steal away its joy: "I know what you're saying, Reverend, but . . ." and the rest of the story is all too familiar. Nothing hinders the flow of God's grace into our lives more than doubt. If unbelief can be driven out by believing, doubt can be discharged by not doubting. The Bible declares that you're gifted. Don't doubt it! Just start looking for your gift. The positive action of searching for God's will drives demon doubt out. You've gotten this far. Don't back out now. Keep going!

C = *Censure all notions of pride or defeat.* Pride and defeat are two serious hurdles to receiving God's grace in the form of spiritual gifts. Paul recognized this problem in Romans 12 and 1 Corinthians 12. He faced both pride and defeat in the use of gifts. He warns that thinking too highly of ourselves and too lowly of others has no place in the body of Christ (see Rom. 12:3; 1 Cor. 13:4; Phil. 2:3-4).

To be gifted by God is a high privilege. To be delivered from sin, liberated from selfishness, and empowered with purposive grace for special ministries is to realize how privileged we are. But this privilege is no warrant for pride, only sacramental obedience. The gifts are not given only to those who show promise or as a reward for obedience. They are given by divine wisdom to serve other members of the body and other people through the body. Why and how God makes choices is known only to God. It's God's divine mystery. Everyone is of equal rank and is equally privileged because everyone is divinely chosen.

Pride has no place; neither does defeat. God does not give us gifts to succeed. God gives gifts to be used. When we sink into a slough of defeat over an apparent failure in the use of our gifts, we damage the body and restrict the flow of God's grace. Excellence is always a worthy goal, but only in the development and application of our gifts. Let us not project this excellence onto results. That is another story altogether. We will get to that in a moment. If persons do not learn from our gift of teaching, that does not mean we did not teach. The hindrance may be in the students. If a person is not healed from our practice of the gift of healing, the barrier to God's healing grace may be somewhere else. If others do not become inspired and encouraged with our gift of exhortation, they are probably at fault. So, let us not retard our efforts because of an apparent lack of success.

E = *Expect God to produce the results.* Results do not belong to us. We do not know how to judge the results. Only God can do that. Our gifted privilege is to use our gifts for God who is the "Lord of the harvest" (Matt. 9:38). We work at the pleasure of the God of results. Paul wrote,

> Therefore, my beloved, as you have always *obeyed,* so now . . . work out your own salvation [wholeness] with fear and trembling; for God is at work in you, both to will and to work for his good pleasure.
> —Philippians 2:12-13, emphasis mine

We seek God's good pleasure. This idea defies the notion of entitlement. The harvest of our efforts is not worthy pursuits, only the privilege and the pleasure of working with and for the God of the harvest.

Many seek from God what they want and what they believe they are entitled to, but sadly and eventually they find they do so at the cost of a vital relationship with God. To seek anything other than God's will and pleasure is to travel a road that leads to certain burnout of faith and joy. We must remember that a spiritual gift is never for the profit or aggrandizement of the gifted but for the glory of God (see 1 Pet. 4:11) and for the edification of the body (see Eph. 4:12). Using our spiritual gifts always produces God's intended results, results that God designs and harvests.

We don't always know the results of our obedience, but we don't have to know to be obedient. Authentic faith—disciplined faith—that puts us in touch with the God who gives gifts also enables us to trust God fully. This includes all that eventuates beyond the joy and splendor of obedience: "To him be the dominion for ever and ever. Amen" (1 Pet. 4:11).

Grace-Gifts Discovery Inventory

Before you take this inventory, please consider four imperatives: (1) Pray sincerely for God's guidance. God wants you to know and use your gifts. (2) Do not relate these to your profession or occupation. (3) Do not consider how you relate to your family or what you do for your family. (4) Make every effort to rank all items *in relationship to* what you have done and experienced within the body of Christ, the church.

If you have no previous experience as a Christian or church member, consider this statement about each item: If I have the opportunity, time, and resources, this describes my inclination. (Then list one of the numbers described below.)

Rank (assign a value to) each of the following statements according to how it describes your experience or strong inclination—not how to make you look good: *Much* (3), *Some* (2), *Little* (1), or *None* (0). Write the number of the value in the blank to the right of the statement.

1. I have a special sense of right and wrong, justice and injustice, and need to express it to others. _____

2. I enjoy working with and spiritually caring for groups of persons. _____

3. It is easy for me to aid persons in learning relevant information about the Bible and Christian living. _____

4. What I understand as divine truth is easy for me to apply to daily living. _____

5. Discovering or recognizing spiritual meanings and divine principles comes easily for me. _____

6. I delight in working with and encouraging depressed or apathetic persons. _____

7. I intuitively spot what is real or phony in other people and situations. _____

8. It is easy and enjoyable to manage my income so that I may give liberally to God's work. _____

163

9. The needs of others, more than my own or my family's, excite me to Christian action. _____

10. Persons with problems and pain attract my attention more quickly than others without apparent needs. _____

11. Other cultures, races, and languages offer no hurdles for my Christian service. _____

12. I bring persons to Christ through my personal efforts. _____

13. I offer friendship and other services to strangers without hesitation and fear. _____

14. I know God actively and purposely works in every event and circumstance. _____

15. I enjoy showing others how they can work for God in the church and the community. _____

16. I am energized by and feel joy when organizing a project, working out details, and getting others in the right places to reach a goal. _____

17. I feel that suffering is one of God's ways of accomplishing a divine purpose in life. _____

18. My prayers are a source of healing for others. _____

19. I pray in words or thoughts that I don't understand. _____

20. I understand and can interpret what others say or pray in words or phrases they do not know as a language. _____

21. Leaving the comforts of home, friends, and my church to serve other Christians elsewhere appeals to me. _____

22. Do I ever wonder how spiritually rewarding it must be not to be married? _____

23. I have a special sense of knowing when others need my prayers. _____

24. I am willing and able to endure any hardship to demonstrate God's love and power to others. _____

25. I enjoy doing most anything for the church and others as long as it serves Christ's purposes. _____

26. I sing praises to God with tunes I've never heard or learned. _____

27. I have a special sense about whether church buildings honor God and aid Christian discipleship. _____

28.. When someone is an obvious victim of an alien evil desire, I feel a strong need to pray for that person's deliverance in the name of Jesus. _____

29. I enjoy debating persons who discredit the value of the church or Christian faith and usually win their esteem. _____

30. I enjoy making others laugh. _____

31. I become aware of surprisingly powerful results from some things I do for God's work. _____

32. A fulfilling life, to me, should be simple and free from obligations that do not directly support kingdom living. _____

33. Definite information and insights about personal and social evils come to me for correcting and guiding the church. _____

34. I enjoy being with and serving the same people over long periods of time. _____

35. I find it easy and enjoyable to explain what the New Testament teaches about Christian living. _____

36. What appears to be a complicated problem for others, I intuitively understand and solve. _____

37. I have special insights to God's will for the church and righteous living that do not always come from studying the Bible or from having a formal education. _____

38. I inspire and motivate others to do things for their spiritual well-being. _____

39. Something inside stirs me to question whether some things are from God, human nature, or evil. _____

40. Giving my time, talents, energy, and money is a cheerful experience of Christian living. _____

41. The main reason I do things for others is to help them in their spiritual growth. _____

42. I have immediate compassion for persons who have spiritual, emotional, or physical pain. _____

43. Ministering to persons who are different from me would be an exciting ministry. _____

44. I get great joy from telling persons who have not professed Christ as Savior how he became my Savior and how he wants to become theirs. _____

45. I sense a special opportunity for ministry when my normal routine is interrupted by guests or strangers. _____

46. I have a blessed assurance that God is involved in everything, small or great, and is working out a divine plan. _____

47. I seem to be "out front" of others in faith ventures, and many follow my example. _____

48. Organizing ideas, people, resources, and schedules is easy and enjoyable for me. _____

49. I identify my pains and tragedies as sharing the suffering of our Lord. _____

50. Because of my specific prayers, certain unhealthy conditions change for the good. _____

51. I experience a spiritual presence and power when I pray or chant in a wordless form. _____

52. When others deliver inspired messages in words and sounds not known by the hearers, I am able to explain. _____

53. I yearn to go to new places to proclaim Christ and to help establish another group of believers. _____

54. I can be a whole person outside a social or legal bond with one person. _____

55. When I hear requests for prayers, I eagerly and immediately begin to pray. _____

56. The prospect of loss or gain because of my faith in Jesus Christ causes me no abiding concern. _____

57. I do most anything that needs to be done because everything is an opportunity to glorify God. _____

58. I easily discern when music is a performance rather
than a spiritual aid to worship. _____

59. I recognize that religious symbols are essential for
enhancing Christian fellowship and worship. _____

60. I know when there are conflicts between evil and
good forces, and I feel that God wants to use me to
eradicate the evil. _____

61. I have such strong feelings about the rightness
of the church's role in the affairs of life, I stand
ready to defend it at whatever cost. _____

62. It is easy for me to spot humor in most situations,
even serious and painful ones. _____

63. I feel mysteriously connected to a divine power when
doing ministries of Christ for others. _____

64. I enjoy having a minimal income and no debts so that
my interests and energies may be put to Christ's
use. _____

65. I am stirred by the modern relevance of biblical
teachings and principles and must speak my mind
about them. _____

66. I find sustained intimacies with a variety of people
easy and enjoyable. _____

67. I devote much time to biblical and spiritual studies
to share with others. _____

68. When I am faced with several options, my choices result
in positive effects. _____

69. I understand and can connect different Bible stories
and teachings without difficulty. _____

70. I consider it important that others gain strength
and comfort from my ministries. _____

71. I am deeply disturbed when something seems wrong, and
exuberant over what seems right, without any apparent
reason for my judgment; eventually, my feelings
prove correct. _____

72. When there is a call for donations, I feel excited
enough to do all I can and, often, more. _____

73. Doing routine tasks is not dull or drudgery for me
if it helps others in their spiritual journey. _____

74. Doing something for persons in nursing homes, hospitals, hospices, and other care-giving places satis-
fies me greatly. _____

75. I have something of value to contribute to peoples
in socioeconomic, racial or language situations radically
different from mine. _____

76. I have deeper feelings for people who need to know
Christ as Savior than for regular church members who
already know Christ. _____

77. I make strangers and newcomers comfortable in my
presence. _____

78. To me, God's will is more important than either a
deliverance from the unpleasant or an acquisition of
the wonderful. _____

79. I have dreams and visions of new ministries that the
church can offer, and I enjoy helping to set long-
range goals for the church's ministries. _____

80. When I take on projects, my planning, detailing, and
supervising result in people friendliness and smooth
operation. _____

81. I see God's powerful love in my sorrow, hardships,
pain, or loss. _____

82. God heals the physically, mentally, socially, financially, or spiritually sick through my efforts. _____

83. I feel spiritually right and normal to pray or to
give praise to God with utterances unlike any language I know. _____

84. I delight in understanding and translating for
others who speak with unintelligible words. _____

85. People accept what I say about spiritual matters
without offering rebuttals. _____

86. The divine purpose of singleness is freedom to give
more time to ministries for our Lord and his church. _____

87. Praying is my most enjoyable spiritual activity. _____

88. I am stubborn and unyielding in my insistence on what Christ means to me and to everyone.

89. I think of cleaning, typing, caring for buildings, ushering, baby-sitting, mowing, setting up chairs, and other acts as significant ways to worship God.

90. My music becomes a God-given means for preparing souls for a special anointing of grace.

91. I feel a special closeness to God when I build, make, or repair something related to the church and God's people.

92. At times I feel that my praying is a battlefield on which evil and good forces are battling for control over someone or some event.

93. I feel like a Christian solider at war with evil, not people.

94. I experience fun and entertainment as vital parts of the practice of Christian faith.

95. Though I do not intend it, extraordinary things occur when I assert special efforts for Christ and his church.

96. God does not want me to have worldly possessions so that the kingdom may claim my time and strength.

97. I experience urges to speak God's message that prove to be timely and needed by others.

98. I find it easy to carry a large amount of concerns for many persons with a variety of needs.

99. I enjoy arduous and long hours of study to make God's word plain and easy to understand for others.

100. The themes of love, righteousness, holiness, peace, and discipleship are easy for me to translate into practical acts of daily Christian living.

101. Meanings and overtones of biblical themes are more important than mere facts, names, or dates.

102. I urge others to believe their sufferings and trials will develop their patience, strength, and hope.

103. I easily detect spiritual truth and error when others see no cause to question the difference. ____

104. I do not care how the church uses my contributions, since what I give is unto God. ____

105. I am satisfied just to serve others, even if I never get recognized for what I do. ____

106. I actually feel the discomforts and pains of others, and I get relief only by doing something to relieve theirs. ____

107. I daydream about living and serving God among people of other nations, races, and cultures. ____

108. I believe that the primary purpose of the church is to win persons to Christ. ____

109. I really love meeting new people and learning about them, and I am eager to greet them to make them feel welcome. ____

110. I know God is real; though circumstances appear hard, cruel, and impossible to others, I relax in knowing that God is in control. ____

111. Others say that my influence has guided them to gain new directions and achievements in life. ____

112. All ministries should be amply planned, sufficiently staffed, and carried out to the fullest detail. ____

113. God uses my sorrows to bring about radical changes for the good of other persons and events. ____

114. Through my counseling, touch, or prayer, illnesses disappear. ____

115. In my private devotions, I pray both with words I understand and with utterances I don't understand. ____

116. I interpret messages from spiritual languages to build up the members of the church. ____

117. I enjoy spending lots of time visiting other churches to aid them in their services to Christ. ____

118. God gives special relief from sexual needs and frustrations to single persons. ____

119. I am moved to pray for others, even though I may not know them, and for conditions about which I know very little or nothing at the time.

120. I prefer dying painfully for Jesus Christ than dying painlessly without knowing him personally.

121. Because of a special closeness I feel to God when I do any kind of work for the church, I am quick to volunteer.

122. When I sing or play music, I feel spiritual energy flowing through me.

123. I am spiritually fulfilled when engaged in creative and artistic physical or manual work for the good of the church.

124. I need to know and to name the demonic force in order to pray or work effectively for its elimination.

125. I view the church as an army of the Lord and myself as a part of its special victory force.

126. I recognize amusing events and statements in the Bible that most people do not see.

127. I experience unexpected and unsolicited inner promptings to do some service for Christ and the church and learn later of unbelievable results.

128. I feel it is important for me to identify with the poor to build their confidence in my service to them.

129. I receive special insights for warnings, cautions, instructions, and encouragements to give to the church for its effectiveness and preservation.

130. I have special feelings for Christians who have strayed and for church members who are inactive.

131. It gives me pleasure to explain God's word in such a way that others learn how to live righteously.

132. I see God's will clearly and how to apply it to personal living and church ministries.

171

133. It is clear to me how biblical teachings relate to universal and timeless needs of human life. ____

134. Through my personal involvement, troubled, depressed, or confused persons receive strength and composure in the Lord. ____

135. I have a special sensing for false teachings, erroneous judgments, and insincere and dishonest behavior. ____

136. My giving as a Christian is determined not by my special interests, ability, or resources but by joy and gratitude. ____

137. People are so important to me that everything I do as a Christian must be done for their good. ____

138. I have strong inclinations toward people with troubles and special needs, and I get special joy from helping them. ____

139. My heart goes out to the unchurched, underprivileged, and others the church is not touching with its gospel of Christ. ____

140. While talking with anyone who appears not to be a Christian, I experience a strong desire to be the one to win him or her to Christ. ____

141. I do not mind and am not afraid to welcome unknown persons into my home. ____

142. Even when wrong prevails and situations threaten with hopelessness, I sense that God's blessing is forthcoming. ____

143. People seek me out to lead them in their faith ventures. ____

144. Carrying the responsibility for organizing group activities toward stated goals is something I enjoy and do well. ____

145. My witness in affliction and troubles has been used of God to lead others to experience the joy of Christ in their hardships. ____

146. Directly through my various efforts, healings occurred that did not come from natural or medical means. ____

147. Praying or praising God in wordless sounds and phrases gives me a sense of unhindered and intimate communication with God. ____

148. I receive direct clarifications of divine messages for the good of the church through persons who, to others, speak in unintelligible gibberish. ____

149. When I visit from church to church and have occasion to speak, I feel a sense of authority in spiritual matters that comes only from God. ____

150. Being single and enjoying it never discounts the value of marriage for others but frees me to serve the church more fully. ____

151. I feel urges to pray for others to be empowered for effective ministries. ____

152. Whatever the costs, I do not hesitate to tell others about God's love in Jesus Christ. ____

153. It does not matter how menial or mundane my task, my joy is doing it for Christ. ____

154. I can tell whether certain hymns and types of music are spiritually suitable for the occasion. ____

155. Engaging my manual skills for Christ and his church is a special form of prayer and ministry for me. ____

156. God uses my obedience to free others of evil forces. ____

157. I think of unbelievers not as enemies but as persons in need of a strong Christian influence and commander. ____

158. I use wholesome jokes and laughable statements to relieve others of pressure, anxiety, or suffering. ____

159. I feel mystically empowered by the presence of God when doing some things that others may consider insignificant, strange, or impossible. ____

160. Having little of this world's goods doesn't make me feel inferior to others or left out of God's grace. ____

How to Score Your Inventory

The numbers in the chart on the next page refer to the numbered inventory items you just ranked (pages 163-173). Look back at the inventory to see the value you assigned to each question, and pencil in that value (3, 2, 1, or 0) next to the number of that question in each box. After listing the 160 values, add your total horizontally for each row in the chart. (Do not include the printed numbers.) Put the sum on the line in the Total column. The sum ranges from 0 to 15.

The total for each row indicates the extent to which you may be gifted or inclined to operate the gift named in the first column of the row. Look to see which gifts have the highest totals. If you recorded a high total for the gift of evangelism, for example, you might pray for ways God can best help you operate that gift. Read Chapter 13, "Discovering Our Gifts," for more clues as to what to do to fully utilize your gift.

The Inventory Scoring Chart is on the next page.

Gifts		Values				Total
Prophecy	1	33	65	97	129	
Pastor	2	34	66	98	130	
Teaching	3	35	67	99	131	
Wisdom	4	36	68	100	132	
Knowledge	5	37	69	101	133	
Exhortation	6	38	70	102	134	
Discernment	7	39	71	103	135	
Giving	8	40	72	104	136	
Helps	9	41	73	105	137	
Mercy	10	42	74	106	138	
Missionary	11	43	75	107	139	
Evangelism	12	44	76	108	140	
Hospitality	13	45	77	109	141	
Faith	14	46	78	110	142	
Leadership	15	47	79	111	143	
Administration	16	48	80	112	144	
Suffering	17	49	81	113	145	
Healings	18	50	82	114	146	
Prayer Language	19	51	83	115	147	
Interpretation	20	52	84	116	148	
Apostle	21	53	85	117	149	
Singleness	22	54	86	118	150	
Intercessory Prayer	23	55	87	119	151	
Martyrdom	24	56	88	120	152	
Service	25	57	89	121	153	
Spirit-Music	26	58	90	122	154	
Craftsmanship	27	59	91	123	155	
Exorcism	28	60	92	124	156	
Battle	29	61	93	125	157	
Humor	30	62	94	126	158	
Miracles	31	63	95	127	159	
Poverty	32	64	96	128	160	

Gifts' Definitions and Biblical References

These definitions have been kept to a minimum amount of words. Elaborations are available in the chapters describing the gifts. Keep in mind the adjective *extraordinary* which should be placed before the word *ability*. Spiritual gifts are superabilities God gives for ministries.

1. *Prophecy.* The ability to link biblical truths and God's will for today's living and to be an instrument for revealing or interpreting historic or current messages from God for righteous and just living in today's world.

> Acts 2:14-36; 11:28; 15:32; 21:10ff.; 21:9-11
> Romans 12:6
> 1 Corinthians 12:10; 14:3, 6, 24ff.
> Ephesians 3:1-6; 4:11-14

2. *Pastor.* The ability to carry varieties of spiritual, physical, and social concerns for groups and individuals and to persist over long periods of time and circumstances with effective caring.

> Matthew 18:12-14   Ephesians 4:11-14
> John 10:1-30   1 Timothy 3:1-7
> Acts 20:28   1 Peter 5:2-4

3. *Teaching.* The ability to discern, analyze, and deliver biblical and other spiritual truths to help others to comprehend and accept the clear calling of God to live justly and righteously.

> Acts 13:1; 18:24-28;   1 Timothy 2:7
>   20:20-21   2 Timothy 1:11
> 1 Corinthians 12:28   James 3:1
> Ephesians 4:11

4. *Wisdom.* The ability to make concrete, practical, and specific applications of divine knowledge received directly from God, from one's spiritual gift of knowledge, or from another's shared gift or gifts.

Acts 6:3, 10; 7:10   Colossians 1:28; 3:16
1 Corinthians 1:18-25,   2 Peter 3:15
    26-27; 3:18-19; 12:18

5. *Knowledge.* The ability to ascertain and to understand the universal and timeless truths of God and to link them with the church in its mission through Christ for justice and righteousness in the world.

Acts 5:1-11   2 Corinthians 11:6
Romans 11:33   Ephesians 3:19
1 Corinthians 12:8   Colossians 2:3

6. *Exhortation.* The ability to counsel, inspire, motivate, encourage, and strengthen others in and through their efforts to live out God's will and calling as Christians in pain or pleasure, want or plenty.

Acts 4:36; 11:19-26; 14:22   1 Timothy 4:13
Romans 12:8   Hebrews 10:25
1 Thessalonians 2:11

7. *Discerning of Spirits.* The ability to differentiate between good and evil, right and wrong, and what is of God, human nature, or evil, and to use this knowledge for the protection and health of the body of Christ.

Matthew 7:6   2 Peter 2:1-3
Acts 5:1-11; 8:22-23   1 John 4:1-6
1 Corinthians 12:10

8. *Giving.* The ability to manage one's resources of income, time, energy, and skills to exceed what is considered to be a reasonable standard for giving to the church, an amount that brings joy and power to do more for further service.

1 Kings 17:8-16   Acts 4:32-37
Mark 12:41-44   Romans 12:8
Luke 8:1-3; 21:1-4   2 Corinthians 8:1-7

9. *Helps.* The ability and eagerness to aid or assist others in need to such an extent that the helper receives as much as the persons helped.

Psalm 21:1	Acts 9:36
Mark 15:41	Romans 16:1-2
Luke 8:2-3	1 Corinthians 12:28

10.[11]*Mercy.* The ability to identify with and actually feel the physical, mental, spiritual, and emotional pain or distress of others and to feel the absolute necessity to do something to relieve them.

Matthew 20:29-34	Acts 11:28-30; 16:33-34
Mark 9:41	Romans 12:8
Luke 10:33-35	

11.[9]*Missionary.* The ability to go beyond race, culture, subculture, creeds, nationality, or life-style to serve the basic human and spiritual needs of certain neglected peoples.

Matthew 25:37-40;	Romans 10:14-17
28:19-20	1 Corinthians 9:19-23
Acts 8:4-8; 13:2-12	

12.[6]*Evangelism.* The ability to give such a persuasive witness to the love of God as expressed in Jesus Christ that it moves others to accept that love and to become disciples of Christ.

Acts 8:5-6; 21:8	1 Timothy 2:7
1 Corinthians 3:5-6	2 Timothy 4:5
Ephesians 4:11	

13.[13]*Hospitality.* The ability to extend caring and sharing to persons (strangers) beyond one's intimate circle to demonstrate and establish the unlimited and inclusive companionship of Christ.

Matthew 25:35	1 Timothy 3:2
Acts 16:14-16	Titus 1:8
Romans 12:13	1 Peter 4:9-10

14.[13]*Faith.* The ability to extend one's basic or saving faith to serve corporate and individual needs specifically related to the life and ministry of the church, the body of Christ.

Matthew 17:19-21	Romans 4:18-21
Mark 9:23	1 Corinthians 12:9
Acts 11:22-24	Hebrews 11

15. *Leadership.* The ability to envision God's will and purpose for the church and to demonstrate compelling skills in capturing the imaginations, energies, skills, and spiritual gifts of others to pursue and accomplish God's will.

Luke 10:16	1 Timothy 3:4; 5:17
Acts 7:10	Titus 3:8, 14
Romans 12:8	Hebrews 13:17

16. *Administration.* The ability to sort out resources and persons for effective church ministries and to organize and implement them into ministry projects until completion with eventful results.

Luke 14:28-30	Romans 12:8
Acts 6:1-7	1 Corinthians 12:28

17. *Suffering.* The ability to endure hardship, pain, and distress with an amount of joy and fortitude to inspire others to endure their suffering and to lead others to accept God's offer of salvation made possible in Christ's suffering.

Matthew 16:24	2 Corinthians 11:23-27; 12:1-10
Mark 8:34	Philippians 1:29ff.
John 18:11	1 Peter 4:12-14
Romans 8:17	

18. *Healings.* The ability to cure or to be cured of ill conditions that hinder effective ministries for Christ, the church, or individuals.

Luke 5:17; 6:19; 9:2,	1 Corinthians 12:9, 28
11, 42	1 Peter 2:24
Acts 3:1-10; 5:12-16	

19. *Prayer-Praise Language.* The ability to pray to or praise God with beneficial wordless phrases or utterances not familiar as a known language, and with such a joy-filled intimacy with Christ that faith is strengthened and ministries become effective.

Acts 2:1-13; 10:44-46;   1 Corinthians 12:10, 28; 13:1; 14:4-5, 22
  19:1-7   Ephesians 6:18
Romans 8:26-27

20.[6] *Interpretation.* The ability to hear, comprehend, and translate spiritual messages given by others in wordless phrases or utterances unfamiliar as a known language or to decipher and translate spiritual messages from another who speaks in a known language but not recognized by the interpreter.

Luke 24:27   1 Corinthians 12:10, 30; 14:5, 13, 27
Acts 2:14-21

21.[5] *Apostle.* The ability to adhere to the personality of Jesus Christ and his tradition of missional itineracy so that one may wield effective spiritual oversight of new people in new places for the purpose of extending Christian ministries for spiritual, just, and righteous living.

Acts 15:1-2   Galatians 2:1-10
1 Corinthians 12:28   Ephesians 3:1-13; 4:11
2 Corinthians 12:12

22.[5] *Singleness.* The ability to offer God and the church a life free from marriage, family responsibilities, and sexual frustrations to spend time and energies necessary for certain Christian ministries.

Isaiah 56:3-5   1 Corinthians 7:7, 27-28, 32-35
Matthew 19:10-12; 22:27-30

23.[9] *Intercessory Prayer.* The ability to know when, and for whom or what to pray with effective results.

Luke 22:41-44   Colossians 1:9-12; 4:12-13
Acts 12:5, 12; 16:25-26   1 Timothy 2:1; 4:5
Romans 8:26-27   James 5:14-16, 17-18

24.[1] *Martyrdom.* The ability to stand firm on divinely inspired convictions and divinely directed ministries without equivocation or ulterior motives.

Acts 6:10, 15; 7:54-60   1 Thessalonians 2:2
1 Corinthians 13:3   1 Timothy 6:12

25.[15] *Service.* The ability to elevate any deed or service that aids the church or another person to a form of worship without concern or desire for rank, popularity, position, or recognition.

Matthew 4:11	Acts 6:1
Mark 1:31	Romans 12:7
Luke 10:40	Galatians 6:2, 10
John 12:2	Titus 3:4

26.¹³ *Spirit-Music.* The ability to create or perform lyrics and musical tunes as messages from God to inspire others to Christian service, to win others to Christ, or to tell the story of God's love and grace.

2 Chronicles 5:11-14	1 Corinthians 14:15
Psalm 57:7-9	Ephesians 5:19

27.⁹ *Craftsmanship.* The ability to use physical materials and artistic skills to create, mold, carve, sculpt, draw, design, paint, repair, or photograph items necessary for spiritual nurture, faith development, and caring ministries.

Exodus 35:20-35; 36:1-3

28.³ *Exorcism.* The ability to use faith, prayers, spirit-music, or other spiritual gifts to liberate persons from debilitating and hindering forces and evil circumstances to free them to use their gifts effectively to serve the body of Christ and others through the church.

1 Samuel 16:14-23	Acts 5:16; 8:6-8; 16:16; 19:11-12
Matthew 8:16-17; 12:43-45	1 Corinthians 2:6-8; 10:20-21
Mark 1:24; 16:17	Ephesians 6:10-18
Luke 9:1, 49-50; 10:17; 11:25	Colossians 1:13-15; 2:20

29.¹ *Battle.* The ability to use spiritual, physical, or psychological energies with righteous force enough to confront and overcome evil that hinders the church's mission to do God's will.

Deuteronomy 31:6	1 Corinthians 16:13
Joshua 1:6-9	Ephesians 6:10-17
2 Samuel 10:12	1 Thessalonians 2:2
Daniel 10:19	1 Timothy 6:12
Acts 23:11	

30.¹⁴ *Humor.* The ability to bring laughter and joy to situations and relationships to relieve tension, anxiety, or conflicts and to heal and free emotions and energies needed for effective ministries.

John 13:6-15   Galatians 5:12
1 Corinthians 12:12-24

31. *Miracles*. The ability to do powerful works that transcend our perception of natural laws and means to free the church or individuals from conditions that restrict needed ministries.

Genesis 18:14   Acts 4:30; 5:1-10; 5:12; 13:11
Mark 9:38-40; 16:17-18   1 Corinthians 2:4; 12:10, 28
Luke 1:37

32. *Voluntary Poverty*. The ability to live a simple, conservative, and unencumbered life free of material responsibilities in order to devote large amounts of time, energy, and skills to essential ministries.

Mark 1:18, 20; 10:21   1 Corinthians 13:3
Acts 2:45; 4:34-35   2 Corinthians 8:9

Bibliography

I am indebted to more authors than space allows me to mention. I list only a few special ones. I do not quote from any of them, but must express gratitude for inspiration derived from their works.

Banks, Robert. *Paul's Idea of Community*. Grand Rapids, MI: Wm. B. Eerdmans Publishing Co., 1980.

Barclay, William. *The Letters to the Corinthians*. Philadelphia: The Westminster Press, 1975. (I refer the reader to other books by Dr. Barclay in the same Daily Bible Series.)

Dunnam, Maxie. *The Workbook of Intercessory Prayer*. Nashville: The Upper Room, 1979.

Galipeau, Steven A. *Transforming Body and Soul*. Mahwah, New Jersey: Paulist Press, 1990.

Hillman, Robert J. *27 Spiritual Gifts*. Melbourne, Australia: The Joint Board of Christian Education, 1986.

Kelsey, Morton. *Tongue Speaking: The History and Meaning of the Charismatic Experience*. New York: Crossroad, 1981.

Kinghorn, Kenneth Cain. *Gifts of the Spirit*. Nashville: Abingdon Press, 1976.

Kittel, Gerhard and Gerhard Friedrich, eds. *Theological Dictionary of the New Testament, Abridged in One Volume*, trans. and abridged by Geoffrey W. Bromiley. Grand Rapids, MI: Wm. B. Eerdmans Publishing Co., 1985.

Koenig, John. *Charismata: God's Gifts for God's People*. Philadelphia: The Westminster Press, 1978.

Kung, Hans. *The Church*. NY: Doubleday, 1976.

Laurentin, Rene. *Catholic Pentecostalism*. Garden City, NY: Doubleday, 1977.

MacGorman, J.W. *The Gifts of the Spirit*. Nashville: Broadman Press, 1980.

Minear, Paul S. *Images of the Church in the New Testament*. Philadelphia: The Westminster Press, 1970.

Moltmann, Jurgen. *The Church in the Power of the Spirit*. New York: Harper & Row, 1977.

Nouwen, Henri J.M. *The Wounded Healer*. Garden City, NY: Doubleday, 1972.

Opsahl, Paul D., ed. *The Holy Spirit in the Life of the Church, from Biblical Times to the Present*. Minneapolis: Augsburg Publishing House, 1978.

Siegel, Bernie S. *Love, Medicine and Miracles*. New York: Harper & Row, 1986.

Snyder, Howard A. *The Problem of Wineskins: Church Renewal in a Technological Age*. Downers Grove, IL: Inter-Varsity Press, 1975. (Also two others: *The Community of the King* (1975) and *The Radical Wesley* (1980).

Stedman, Ray C. *Body Life* (rev. ed.) Ventura, CA: Regal Books, 1979.

Stott, John R.W. *God's New Society: The Message of Ephesians*. Downers Grove, IL: Inter-Varsity Press, 1980.

Sweet, Leonard I. *New Life in the Spirit*. Philadelphia: The Westminster Press, 1982.

Thayer, Joseph H. *Greek-English Lexicon of the New Testament*. Grand Rapids, MI: Baker Book House, 1977.

Thielicke, Helmut. *The Evangelical Faith, Vol. 3*. Grand Rapids, MI: Wm. B. Eerdmans Publishing Co., 1982.

Tuttle, Robert G. *The Partakers*. Nashville: Abingdon Press: 1974.

Wagner, C. Peter. *Your Spiritual Gifts Can Help Your Church Grow*. Ventura, CA: Regal Books, 1979.

Wagner, James K. *Blessed to Be a Blessing*. Nashville: The Upper Room, 1980.

About the Author

Dr. Charles V. Bryant is a member of the North Carolina Conference
of The United Methodist Church. He has served churches in Ohio,
North Carolina, and in England at Northwood, Middlesex, and
Middlesborough on Teeside. He served as an associate director of the
North Carolina Conference Council on Ministries from 1982–88.

Dr. Bryant is a graduate of the University of Cincinnati, The
Divinity School of Duke University, and Drew University Theological
School, where he earned his Doctor of Ministry degree.

The author has conducted over 400 workshops on spiritual gifts
for seven denominations and in fifteen states. He is also a featured
lecturer on the new Internet distant learning project, "Nicodemus,"
with the Southeastern Jurisdiction Office of Communication.

Dr. Bryant and his wife, Wanda, live in Oriental, North Carolina,
and may be reached at cbryant@coastalnet.com, (252) 249-1669, or
327 Wiggins Point Road, Oriental, North Carolina 28571.